THE MANY HUES OF ENGLISH

THE

A B C D E F G H I J K L M
N O P Q R S T U V W X Y Z

MANY HUES

A B C D E F G H I J K L M N
O P Q R S T U V W X Y Z

OF ENGLISH

a b c d e f g h i j k l m n o p q r s t u v w x y z

by MARIO PEI

1967

ALFRED · A · KNOPF New York

Library of Congress Catalog Card Number: 67–18609

THIS IS A BORZOI BOOK
PUBLISHED BY ALFRED A. KNOPF, INC.

FIRST EDITION

The author gratefully acknowledges permission to use his previously published material:

Chapter 1 is based on "English for Americans," *Holiday* (July 1955), which later appeared in *Talking Your Way Around the World*, Harper & Brothers, 1961.
Chapter 3 blends two articles: "Your Speech Says More Than You Think," *Think Magazine* (January 1958), © Copyright 1958 by International Business Machines, and "What Did He Say?" *Police* (September–October 1959), © Copyright 1959 by Charles C. Thomas, Publisher.
Chapter 4 is based on "Pidgin English Around the World," *Tomorrow* (January 1950), Copyright 1950 by Garrett Publications, Inc., and later reprinted as "World Pidgins" in *Talking Your Way Around the World*, Harper & Brothers, 1961.
Chapter 5 appeared originally in *Tomorrow* (January 1951), Copyright 1951 by Garrett Publications, Inc.
Chapter 6 is based on an article in *Challenge, The Magazine of Economic Affairs* (June–July 1958), © Copyright 1958 by *Challenge*.
Chapter 7 originally appeared in the *Saint Anthony Messenger* (August 1946), Copyright 1946 by *Saint Anthony Messenger*.
Chapter 8 is based on "Reading in Different Languages," an address delivered before the Reading Institute of Temple University, January 25, 1962, and originally published in the *Proceedings of the Annual Reading Institute*, Vol. 1, 1962. Excerpted from *International Language Review* (April–June 1963).
Chapter 10 is excerpted from the review of *Leave Your Language Alone* by Robert A. Hall. *Symposium*, IV, 2 (November 1950), Copyright 1950 by *Symposium*.
Chapter 11 is excerpted from the review of *Chamber of Horrors* by 'Vigilans.' *American Speech*, XXVIII, 3 (October 1953), Copyright 1953 by Columbia University Press.
Chapter 12 is excerpted from a review of *The Concise Usage and Abusage* by Eric Partridge. *American Speech*, XXX, 3 (October 1955), © Copyright by Columbia University Press.
Chapter 13 is excerpted from a review of *A Dictionary of American-English Usage* by Margaret Nicholson and *A Dictionary of Contemporary American Usage* by Bergen Evans and Cornelia Evans. *Saturday Review* (August 31, 1957), © Copyright by *Saturday Review*.
Chapter 14 is excerpted from a review of *Webster's Third New International Dictionary, Unabridged. The New York Times Book Review* (April 7, 1963), © Copyright 1945–1963 by The New York Times Company.
Chapter 15 is based on "The Dictionary as a Battlefront," *Saturday Review* (July 21, 1962), © Copyright 1962 by *Saturday Review*.
Chapter 16 is based on "A Loss for Words," *Saturday Review* (November 14, 1964), © Copyright by *Saturday Review*.
Chapter 17 originally appeared in *Tomorrow* (August 1950), Copyright 1950 by Garrett Publications, Inc.
Chapter 18 originally appeared under the title "Our Influence on Italian" in *American Speech* (December 1950), Copyright 1950 by Columbia University Press.
Chapter 21 originally appeared in the *Modern Language Journal* (January 1947), Copyright 1947 by *Modern Language Journal*.
Chapter 22 originally appeared in *Saturday Review* (January 15, 1966), © Copyright 1966 by *Saturday Review*.
Chapter 23 originally appeared under the title "A World Language?" in *Television Age* (July 4, 1966), © Copyright 1966 by *Television Age*.
Chapter 24 is based on "English in 2061: A Forecast," *Saturday Review* (January 14 1961), © Copyright 1961 by *Saturday Review*.

Foreword

This volume represents a cross section of one man's thinking, at various stages of his adult career, about his adopted language—a language that impressed him from his earliest contacts with it by reason of its resiliency and effectiveness, its unesthetic sounds and strange spellings, its conciseness and precision, its looseness of structure and hyperbolic conveyance of thought, its wealth of borrowings and international sources, its supercilious insularity and insistence upon having its own way, its orderliness in the midst of supreme disorder, the affection and reverence, the unconcern and disrespect bestowed upon it by its speakers, the attention and serious study, the dislike and contempt mixed with envy and admiration to which it is subjected by speakers of other tongues.

Most of the chapters are reproductions, with modifications, of articles and reviews composed between 1946 and 1966. The reader may come across passages that seem written from different points of view. This, to my mind, is a writer's right and prerogative. As the language grows and unfolds, so does the mentality of its speakers, and the writer, for better or worse, is one of those speakers. Many controversies have arisen in the course of the last twenty years, and as the issues have developed and clarified themselves, a firmer stand has become necessary. Facts are facts, and they seldom change; but new light may be cast upon existing facts. Opinions are subject to the facts as we see them at any given time, and to the lights that may illuminate one or another fact previously left in the penumbra.

The most factual section of our book is the initial one,

dealing with the varieties of the English language. Here change comes with relative slowness. The chapters dealing with the flux of English point to some of the vexing problems of the language, and discuss human attitudes and reactions to these problems. What is probably the most absorbing of the issues, that of usage and the dictionary, is then spotlighted. Next comes a section devoted to other languages and their speakers, what they have gotten from us and how they have liked it. Last of all, comes a collection of chapters dealing with probable or possible future developments, both for what concerns the language itself, shorn of its international contacts, and for its potentialities in a world-wide role.

While individual credit lines and copyright notices appear elsewhere, this is a good opportunity to express my appreciation, en bloc, to the numerous magazines (and one publishing house) that have extended permission to re-use material that first appeared in their pages. This expression of gratitude goes out especially to *Saturday Review, The New York Times Book Review, Tomorrow, American Speech, Holiday, Challenge, Think, Police, Modern Language Journal, Symposium, Saint Anthony Messenger, International Language Review, Television Age,* and Harper & Row.

M. P.

CONTENTS

PART ONE

a b c d e f g h i j k l m n o p q r s t u v w x y z

THE VARIETIES OF
ENGLISH

ENGLISH IS THE MOTHER TONGUE OF NEARLY
*three hundred million people—one out of every ten of the
globe's inhabitants. Only Chinese outstrips it in number of
native speakers. In addition, it is official, co-official, or semi-
official in countries numbering well over seven hundred million.
At least one hundred million more people speak and understand
it in forms ranging all the way from the correct, perhaps over-
literary version taught in the schools of continental Europe to
the various pidgins that infest parts of Asia, Africa, and particularly New Guinea and the South Seas. This means that
roughly one out of every three persons in the world is directly
or indirectly accessible by means of English, and the distribution
of English over the globe is such as to make it by far the most
ubiquitous of the world's chief languages, with only French,
Spanish, and Portuguese even remotely approaching its distri-
butional effectiveness.*

*A world-wide language of this type is naturally subject to
dialectalization, and the only wonder is that English is not more
heavily segmented than it actually is.*

*The following four chapters endeavor to give some idea of the
varieties of English—the two chief subdivisions, British and
American; the smaller varieties represented by the English of
Canada, South Africa, New Zealand, and Australia; the further
subdivision, for purposes of illustration, of our own American
English into regional varieties and immigrant dialects; and the
forms of pidgin English that have developed in countries of
other speeches as a result of past colonization and past and
present commercial, religious, political, and military activities
on the part of English speakers.*

CHAPTER ONE

A B C D E F G H I J K L M N O P Q R S T U V W X Y Z

The Two Mainstreams

The tourist bus had finally reached Stratford on Avon. We got off before the inn where we were scheduled to have lunch, and strolled in. After our three-hour ride, we felt the need of rest rooms; in fact, some of us even wanted to wash our hands. There were apparently no rest rooms in the inn. In vain we looked for such familiar signs as "Men," "Women," "Ladies," "Gentlemen," or even the euphemistic "He," "She," "Comfort Station," "Powder Room," "Lounge." In desperation we inquired. There was a trace of ironic condescension in the clerk's voice as he replied: "Why, sir, the cloakroom is out in the entrance hall. It's plainly marked. I don't see how you could have missed it."

Here is the key to George Bernard Shaw's famous utterance to the effect that "Britain and America are two countries separated by the same language." It is perfectly true that there are differences in the pronunciation of individual words (schedule and clerk, in the opening paragraph, are two cases in point; to the British, and even to a few Americans, the first is "shedule"; no American, to my knowledge, goes along with "clark"); there are variations in spelling (cheque, labour, travelled, kerb, tyre, jewellery are only a few of the British versions); there are sometimes vast differences of intonation. But the real rub, the thing that makes you feel like a foreigner in an English-speaking land, is the words and combinations of words that are used with different meanings.

Often the difference lies merely in the choice of words that have the same meaning in both divisions of the Anglo-Saxon world: "Keep Britain tidy!", "Keep America clean!"; "Give the lad a shilling!", "Give the boy a quarter!". We use *tidy* and *lad;* the British use *clean* and *boy.* But we don't use them in the same contexts.

The difference of wording is often indicative of a trait of national psychology. "Perhaps the finest made" says a British magazine ad for a certain brand of raincoat. What American advertiser would inject the note of doubt (more precisely understatement) betokened by that "perhaps"?

Non-linguistic symbols of the difference, such as the cut-away coat, bowler hat, and tightly rolled umbrella of the British "black-coated employee" as against the gray flannel suit and slim tie of the American "junior executive" need not concern us for our present purpose. Similar, and often far vaster differences appear in other lands; but the other lands do not purport to speak the same language and share a common literature, tradition, and cultural background. In the midst of similarities, incongruities and discrepancies strike you harder. That is why an American, lulled into a sense of false security by an English breakfast that so closely resembles his own, finds it more difficult to adjust to diverging British customs than to those of a land where everything is strange, and the first thing that puts you on your guard is the strange tongue you hear spoken all around you.

§   §   §

Every serious, up-to-date linguistic manual insists that there is only one English language, and that the divergences between the English of Britain and that of America are purely dialectal. Earlier linguists, and even laymen, took a different view. H. L. Mencken popularized *The American Language,* but long before that the Fowlers, in their *The King's English*

(1906), asserted that the two English languages are fine, each in its own sphere, but that they are best kept apart.

Probably the earliest recognition of the difference between British and American English is a review written in 1756 by Samuel Johnson of a book by an American-born author, in which the great authority on language denounces the "mixture of American dialect" as a "tract of corruption." By 1778 further notice was taken of the "language of the United States," and by the beginning of the nineteenth century the language of the former colonies was described by some British writers as being as far removed from English as Italian is from Latin, with the further comment that it was monotonous, nasal, and flat. The fact that the speech of Cromwell's Puritans had been similarly described many decades earlier by supporters of Charles I leads one to suspect that it was the speech of New England rather than that of the South that was being referred to. But in addition, an English Annual of 1808 speaks of "the torrent of barbarous phraseology from America, threatening to destroy the purity of the English language." Here the reference is probably to specific American words and coinages, such examples as *raccoon* and *opossum, tomahawk* and *wigwam, big drink* and *to liquor up.* Twenty years later, Webster's first American dictionary offered some twelve thousand such words which had not appeared in Johnson's or any other English dictionary. By the middle of the nineteenth century, such English writers as Dickens, Mrs. Trollope, and Sir Richard Burton did not hesitate to call American English "barbarous" and to hurl thunderbolts at such expressions as *to fix, to notify,* and *fellow countryman.*

Americans did not hesitate to talk back. While certain of our early linguists replied, with some justification, that American English was less corrupt than British English, and closer to Elizabethan and Shakespearean standards, our politicians, both in State legislatures and in Congress, advocated that "American" be declared the official language of the American Union. As late as 1920 someone went to the trouble of coining and proposing the adjective "United-statish." Fortunately nothing came of all this.

But the differences remain, to haunt both native speakers of English and foreigners. The latter, in fact, take a certain malicious glee in pointing them out. They hang out signs offering to teach English in three months, American in two, or informing the tourist that "English is spoken here, American understood." One Italian guide to American English has on its jacket a variety of highly colloquial expressions such as "Scram!", "Skip it ", "In the bag," "Hiya kid!", "lousy," then asks: "What sort of language is this? It is American, a language that is not at all English." The English themselves are not above putting on their cinema marquees: "American Western film—English subtitles."

But the appearance of such exaggerated forms of low humor ought not to blind us to the fact that there are certain fundamental differences between British and American English, and that these differences far transcend the lesser divergences appearing among American varieties (Eastern, Southern, Midwestern; Brooklynese, Charlestonese, Bostonese) or among the far more divergent British dialects (Cockney, Yorkshire, Devonshire, or even Scots, Irish, and Welsh uses of English).

The British are more fortunate than we in having some sort of unofficial standard, the King's (or Queen's) English, which is the usage of the more educated Londoners, and which generally appears in the speech of BBC announcers. This is neither the semi-incomprehensible Oxford accent (a class slang, evolved in university circles), nor the familiar London Cockney of *Pygmalion*—a lower-class dialect, or rather two local lower-class dialects, separated by the Thames. The King's English, an object of awe and reverence to its speakers, is something that has evolved ever since the days of Chaucer out of a mixture of Southern and East Midland dialects, refined and purified by centuries of parliamentary and court usage. It falls pleasantly upon the ear (even the American ear), with its soft but expressive modulation, its wide range of pitch, and its clipped but precise utterance.

Its phonetic qualities are unmistakable. Its intonation is such as to give away its speaker at the end of his first sentence. It has its own rhythm and rate of speed. Among its grosser phonetic features (and note that most of them appear also in one or another American dialect) are the use of a broad *ah*-sound in words like *bath* and *ask;* the open *o* of *pot* and *sorry* (somewhat like the *aw* of *awful* cut short); an *ow*-like quality for the so-called "long *o*" of *most* and *bone,* with a corresponding modification in the *ow*-sound of *how* and *about;* an explosive quality to final consonants, which Americans as often as not pronounce in implosive fashion, not really releasing the final consonant sound of *sit, sip, sick;* and a vanishing *r* before consonants and at the end of words, so that *farther* comes out as *fahthuh,* and *part* as *paht.* Along with this, there is a strong tendency to efface unstressed vowels and even syllables, so that *interesting* comes out as *intresting,* and *necessarily* as *necessrly;* this also means that the secondary stress of long words, so dear to American speakers, becomes non-existent. In personal and place names, the ultimate results are often quite surprising: what looks like *Leicester* turns out to be *Lester, Auchinlek* becomes *Afleck, Marjoribanks* comes out as *Marchbanks,* and *Saint Osyth* and *Saint Olav* appear in spoken form as *Toosey* and *Tooley.* Americans are sometimes the unconscious victims of this British tendency; their *Boston,* named after an English city, was once *Saint Botolph's Town,* and *Wooster* seems to be a typical British cut-down version of *Worcester.*

A *Dictionary of British Pronunciation with American Variants* shows some divergence in twenty-eight per cent of the words. Americans are more inclined to a spelling pronunciation; Englishmen do not seem to mind how much their speech diverges from the common spelling. Consider the following examples:

Spelling	American Pronunciation	British Pronunciation
clerk	clerk	clark
Derby	Derby	Darby
been	bin	been (here the general trend is reversed)
lieutenant	lieutenant	leftenant (save in the Royal Navy)
nephew	nefew	nevew
schedule	skedule	shedule (the British pronunciation, surprisingly, is making headway in America)
figure	figyure	figger (as above)
leisure	leezhur	lezhur
either, neither	eethur, neethur	eye-thur, neye-thur
tomato	tomayto	tomahto

Differences in accentuation are common: in British English, *primarily* and *gárage* have the stress on the first syllable, *fináncier* and *labóratory* on the second, *papá* and *mamá* on the last. Our *specialty* is their *speciálity*, with stress on the *a*.

The written language shows such differences in spelling that it is practically impossible to go through a single written page without becoming aware of the nationality of the writer. It is not merely a question of individual British words, like *programme, grey, gaol* (a far cry from our *jail*), and *waggon*. There are entire classes of suffixes that change appearance from one side of the Atlantic to the other. Our *-er* words of the type of *center* and *theater* show *-re* in British usage (*theatre* and *centre* were common with us until a few decades ago; the same applies to the doubling of the *l* in *travelled, travelling, traveller*, and similar words). Where America generally uses *-ction* Britain uses *-xion* (*inflexion, connexion*). *Honour, labour, flavour, colour* are such dead giveaways that a whodunit was once written about a Britisher who was supposed to have committed suicide after writing a note to the effect that he could not bear the blot upon his "honor" (literally, no Britisher would be caught dead having used that spelling; and have you noticed on British films "Colour by Technicolor"?). More subtle are *pretence, defence, licence* ("Licence for Marriage" says Queen Eliza-

beth II's legal certificate of wedlock to Count Mountbatten).
Also hard to detect are words in *-ize, -ization,* where the
British follow the French practice of using a voiced *s* as
against our more phonetic *z* (*specialise, organisation*).

§   §   §

But the real difference between the two languages lies in the
field of words and word meanings. H. W. Horwill, in his
Anglo-American Interpreter (1939), brought out a very long
list of outstanding differences between British and American. The number has, if anything, increased since then, even
while some of the words of one group have become more
familiar to the speakers of the other.

Some of the divergences are such that you can find yourself suddenly at a loss in the midst of a perfectly satisfactory
conversation. A strange word, a subtle semantic difference,
can give you the impression that your interlocutor has
lapsed into double talk.

There is the case, reported in the press, where an American theatrical producer (in Britain, by the way, he would
be a "manager"; "producer" in British means "director" in
American) received a cable from his British agent about the
opening of his show in London: "Show a success; am posting notices". The second part of this message, in American
parlance, means that the show is closing. Frantically he
cabled back: "Why should a successful play be closing?" All
the Englishman meant was that he was mailing some rave
reviews, obtained, no doubt, from a "press cutting agency"
("clipping bureau" to Americans).

An urgent British government request for some thousands
of bushels of "corn" to feed liberated populations at the
close of the war led the American government to ship just
that—corn, instead of the wheat required by the British.
Had they wanted corn, they would have called for "maize,"
or specified "Indian corn."

No field escapes confusion. By this time, everyone knows
that American gas is British petrol, and an American truck

a British lorry. But there is ever so much more to automotive terminology! A few samples:

American	British	American	British
sedan	saloon	station wagon	shooting brake; estate car
mini car	bubble car		
trailer	caravan	truck trailer	articulator
dump truck	tipping lorry	bookmobile	traveling library
hood	bonnet	top	roof; hood
fender	mudguard wing	trunk compartment	boot
defroster	demister	windshield	windscreen
		crankcase	sump
		muffler	silencer
		directional sign	trafficator
wrench	spanner	flashlight	torch
signboard	hoarding		
ground a wire	earth a wire	private garage	lock-up garage (pronounce GAR-age, please)
highway	carriage way	shoulder	verge (on heath)
private road	unadopted road	detour	diversion
sharp curve, U-turn	hairpin bend	landslide	landslip
fallen rock	loose chippings	traffic circle	roundabout, circus
inner loop	ring road	overpass	flyover
double parking	double banking		
motorist's right-of-way	precedence	pedestrian right-of-way	zebra crossing
traffic merging from left	left coming	road under repairs	road up
dim your headlights	dip your lamps	fill your battery	top off your accumulator
left side of car	near side	right side of car	offside
demonstration	trial run	drive it yourself	self-drive hire car
no prior offenses	clean licence	to drive a taxi	to drive for hire

A "patrolman" in Britain is an agent of the Royal Automobile Club (similar to our A.A.A.), who patrols the roads and helps out stranded motorists. Even more misleading is a "redcap", who in Britain is not a porter, but an M.P., or military policeman.

An excursion into the advertising pages of a British magazine informs us that the British speak of "tubs" rather than "jars" of face cream, and that hair affected by dandruff is "scruffy." A shaving cream is described as "superfatted." For a "dry shaver" (electric razor) there are "mains," "onlets," and "power points" rather than sockets or outlets. We rent things and hire people; they rent only real estate, and hire everything else. "Hire purchase" is our installment plan. At a "chemist's" (drugstore) you may purchase certain medical preparations (patent medicines). In Britain you may buy a "weathercoat" (but "raincoat" is concurrently used), as well as "bespoke" (custom-made) footwear from your local "stockist" (retailer). Pipe tobacco may be obtained in "fob-pocket tins" (who in America remembers fob pockets?). "Tin" is the word universally used in Britain for what to us is a can, or at the most a tin can, but that is not likely to throw anyone off. More to the point, in the realm of foods, are the "biscuits" which mean crackers, the "dessert" which usually means fruit ("sweet" for dessert would not mislead us, however), the "Wimpy" which is a close relative to the American hamburger, the "chips" for French fries, the "aubergine" which is an eggplant, the "joint" which is a roast. "Gobstopper" for jawbreaker may be set down as slang, but there is nothing slangy about "tripe 'n onions," a "banger," or a "treacle tart," while an "American salad" is something quite unknown in America, like the *americano al selz* aperitif of Italy. "Grilled bread" for toast and "bring to *the* boil" do not seriously bother us.

Political campaigns and British courtroom scenes on TV have familiarized us with a good deal of the British legal terminology. Most of us know that a British candidate "stands," does not run, for office; that you actually stand on a British witness stand, which makes the order to "stand down" after you have given your testimony quite logical; that where we have attorneys and counsel they have barristers and solicitors; that the audience is told to "be upstanding" when the bewigged and black-robed judge comes into the courtroom. "Death duty" for inheritance tax, "interfered with" for "molested" (both euphemisms for sexually assaulted or raped), "wagering" or "gaming" for gambling, "assurance" for insurance, present no real semantic problems in their normal contexts. Neither do the names of various shops, "fishmonger," "ironmonger" (hardware store), "sweet shop" (candy or pastry shop). "Cinema" (or "flicks") for movies, "jumble sale" for rummage sale, "dustbin" for ashcan, "infants' school" for kindergarten, even "wage packet" for pay envelope do not lend themselves to serious misunderstanding.

But "dustman" for garbage collector, "mist" for light fog rather than drizzle, "creek" for an inlet of the sea, "butter muslin" for cheesecloth, "gym shoes" for sneakers, the British use of the terms "apartment" and "flat," may throw us. Especially deadly are "underground" for our subway and "subway" for our underpass, the British telephone operator's "You're through!" for "You're connected!" We are accustomed by this time to "wireless" for radio, and most of us have seen enough British films to know that in Britain it's "telly," not TV. Not all of us, on the other hand, know that in Britain the announcer or newscaster is a "newsreader."

To the linguist, though perhaps not to the layman, there is special interest in those words and phrases the use of which identifies the speaker as belonging to one or another area of the English-speaking world. It's not only a matter of "lads," "chaps," and "types" as against "boys," "fellows," and "guys," or of "holiday" *versus* "vacation." It's the subtle feature of "posting a reply-paid letter" instead of mailing a pre-paid or stamped envelope; of "ringing" someone up as against "calling" him up, of "got" as against "gotten," of "Has he red hair?" against "Does he have red hair?", of "filling up" a form rather than filling it out, of living "in" (rather than "on") a street, and traveling "in" (rather than "on") a train, of selling "by" rather than "at" retail, of having a lease "of" rather than "on" life, of getting "through" rather than "by," of "that is all there is about (rather than "to") it."

§ § §

We have rather carefully eschewed two areas of speech: that which covers objects and institutions that appear in one country and not in the other ("mild and bitter," "shandy," "stone ginger" in a British pub, for instance, or the colloquial use of "bob," "quid," "pony," "monkey" to denote various amounts of British currency, for which our closest counterparts would be "two bits," "buck," "C," "grand," in American currency); and the outright slang of the two lands, not on a limited local, but on a nationwide scale. Here would be such terms as "to cheek" and "to chivvy" (to sass and to chisel), "bear garden" (roughhouse), "chucker-out" (bouncer), "sitter-in" (baby-sitter), "toffee-nosed" (stuck-up), "to plough" (to flunk a student). These two divisions of language could easily fill an entire book.

It is, however, a fully established fact that under late-twentieth-century conditions the Queen's English and the American language are tending to converge again into a single mainstream. As cinema, wireless, telly, and Telstar continue their relentless course, the speech habits of Britain are brought to the notice of American speakers, and those of America to the British. Interborrowings have been going on ever since the two forms began to diverge. "Reliable," "talented," "influential," "lengthy," even "Oh, yeah?" and "Come again?" came to Britain from America. "Swank," "spoof," "click," "wind up," "tell off," "take a dim view," "have had it" came to America from Britain. However picturesque the differences may be, they are incidental, not basic. The written language, despite minor spelling differences, is the same. The literature is common to all lands that describe themselves as English-speaking. Even the popular tongue shows *relatively* few differences.

While we wait for the two mainstreams to converge, we can therefore stress the fundamental unity of the English language. Variety there is and always will be. But variety is the spice of life, and the English language is nothing if not alive.

CHAPTER TWO

A B C D E F G H I J K L M N O P Q R S T U V W X Y Z

The Rivulets

The two mainstreams of English are touched at different points along their course by many minor streams. Chief among these are the tongues of three Commonwealth countries where English speakers form an absolute majority of the population (Australia, New Zealand, Canada) and another (South Africa) where they are such a considerable minority that their language can in no way be described as a mere colonial offshoot or a pidgin. All diverged from the mainstreams in the late eighteenth or early nineteenth centuries. The big Anglo-American split antedates them all by at least one hundred fifty years.

Australian, New Zealand, and South African English stem directly from the English of Britain. Canadian English may more properly be described as stemming from American, or at least as a blend of the two mainstreams. The first English speakers to reach Canada in considerable numbers were the American Tories who did not care to sever their connections with the British Crown after the American Revolution. In the Atlantic coastal regions and in the central provinces of Canada they were joined by numerous new entrants from England and Scotland. The Canadian West is linguistically a blend of earlier Canadians, new immigrants from the British Isles, and people from every country in Europe. But the linguistic tone of Canada had already been set by the beginning of the nineteenth century, and since then, in spite of imperial affiliations, the geographical proximity of the United States and the open border between the two countries has led to American rather than British influence in the Canadian speech.

A Canadian sometimes gets mistaken for an American in Britain and for an Englishman in the United States. It is symptomatic that Canadian naval officers were warned shortly after the war to drop their "phony English accents." So far as the sounds of the language are concerned, the average American has as much difficulty in distinguishing a Canadian as the average Canadian has in distinguishing an American. About the only truly outstanding phonological feature by which you can tell a Canadian from a Midwesterner is the use of a modified *ow*-sound in *house* or *about* that appears in the speech of most parts of Britain and in several American localities, notably Maryland and Virginia. But the American use of the modified *ow* is surrounded by Southern speech features that are altogether lacking in Canadian pronunciation.

Not quite the same applies to spelling and vocabulary. The Canadian generally joins America in such words as *tire* and *wagon,* but Britain in the long list of words where the *l* may be doubled (*woollen, travelled*) and the telltale *-our* suffix (*honour, labour*). The last letter of the alphabet is *zee* to Americans, but *zed* to Canadians, as to Britishers. This little peculiarity served as a shibboleth for the draft authorities of both countries during the war.

Cultural and commercial exchanges between the United States and Canada are such that it is the American rather than the British vocabulary that triumphs. A British-compiled *Dictionary of Canadianisms* containing approximately a thousand terms lists only three dozen or so that are not common to the United States as well, and most of them are jocular localisms concerning the people across the border or across the ocean. The Canadians sometimes refer to Old Glory as "the Gridiron," and to the Glorious Fourth as "Rebel picnic." They join us in the use of the dollar rather than the pound as a unit of currency, but sometimes refer to it slangily as a "toadskin." A recent arrival from the British Isles may be humorously referred to as an "improved Britisher" or "new chum" (but this term appears also in Australia and New Zealand). One outstanding Canadianism is "to stand sam" for "to treat." Other expressions are purely local, and many of them can be found in use across the border ("unbleached American" for Negro, "to have the sun in one's eyes" for to be under the influence of liquor, "sun-downer" for tramp, "pump-sucker" for teetotaler, "out of sight" for in good health, "jig" for day's work, "devil-dodger" for parson, "bagman" for traveling salesman, "blue ruin," "dog's nose," "forty-rod," "snow-broth" for various kinds of alcoholic beverages).

All in all, the linguists seem justified in pronouncing Canadian a branch of American English, one that would draw little attention if it were on our side of the border. This, of course, does not apply to the Canadian French which is the mother tongue of about five million Canadians (Canadian speakers of English number about twelve million) concentrated mostly in the Province of Quebec, but with ramifications to Ontario on the west and to New England, particularly Maine and Rhode Island, on the south. French-Canadian English, in cases where the French-Canadian speaker has not had thorough English training in the schools, partakes of some of the characteristics of a pidgin, with abundant mispronunciation, frequent injection of French words into the English phrase (lots of English gets into the French of these speakers, too), and picturesque loan translations, such as "I am unbuttoned" for "I have been found out," "That's another pair of shoes" for "That's a horse of another color," and "You can work us as fifty by ourselves, but never one in a bunch."

§   §   §

South African English is beset on its own soil by competition from Afrikaans, a language that is an offshoot of the early Dutch brought in by the ancestors of the Boers, and from the numerous African Negro languages, mostly of the Bantu family, that are spoken by the majority of the population. It is a little difficult to unscramble English from Afrikaans speakers, as a great many are bilingual, but it is estimated that out of the South African Union's population of seventeen million no more than one million have English as their mother tongue, as against two and a half million speakers of Dutch-based Afrikaans.

The South African English accent is described as a mixture of Cockney, Scots, and Afrikaans, with a higher pitch and more distinct pronunciation of unaccented syllables than British English, and a few phonetic variants ("pen" and "keb" for pin and cab, and the ubiquitous Cockney "lidy," "pile" for lady, pale). It is somewhat regretfully reported by British linguistic researchers that Afrikaans is gaining over English, and endowing it with an abundance of loan translations of the type of "by [for "in"] the house," "We'll trek at schimmel day," "The river is down," "He threw me with a rock." Straight loan words from Afrikaans are numerous: in addition to the *trek* and *schimmel day* (start out and daybreak) above, are such terms as *erf* (farmyard), *lager* (camp), *schelm* (rascal), *sluit* (gully), *morgen* (land measure), *kloof* (depression between hills), *veld* (open country), *baas* (this gives rise to our own *boss*), *kranz* (precipice), *kraal* (fenced field, village; but this was previously borrowed by the Boers from the Portuguese *curral,* which is the same word as our own Spanish-derived *corral*), *dopper* (conservative), *springbok* (raw recruit; taken from the name of one of the many African antelopes), *uitlander* (foreigner), *lekker* (nice), *strandloper* (beachcomber), and, of course, *apartheid. Inspan* (to harness) and *bywoner* (poor white) are of Dutch-Afrikaans origin. *Commando,* which first arose in South Africa to denote white raiders who carried out reprisals against the raiding blacks, is of Portuguese origin. There are geographical terms that remind one of the familiar Dutch words of our own Hudson Valley: *daal* (valley), *dorp* (village), *fontein* (fountain, spring), *hoek* (hook), *kop* or *kopje* (head).

The South African native languages contribute to South African English in rather generous measure. *Impi* is a Zulu army, from the days of Cetewayo and King Chaka. *Donga, indaba, amasi* are Bantu for gully, council, sour milk. *Inkoos* or *inkosi*, the Zulu word for chief, gets to mean bestower of benefits and is often used for thanks, or as acknowledgment of a favor received. *Knobkerry* and *assegai*, two of the native weapons, come respectively from Hottentot and Berber, far to the north. *Ayah, nooi*, and *sambriero* (nursemaid, girl, straw hat) are of Portuguese origin. Malay contributes *atjar* or *blatjang* (pickles), *baatje* (jacket), *sjambok* (leather whip), *pondok* (hut). *Goniv* and *goniva* (thief and loot) seem to be of Hebrew origin. There is a use of *to jump*, in the sense of to steal, and *trap*, for stool pigeon, that probably go back to British cant. *Shebeen* (speakeasy), *blerry* (no good), *donner* (to beat up) are probably of Irish or Scots Gaelic origin.

The vocabulary of racial segregation includes *European* or *white; colored* (East Indian or other Oriental, half-breed) and *native* (all blacks; illogically, a black African from beyond the South African border is a *foreign native*). *Non-white* is often used to include both *colored* (in the definition above) and *native*. Curiously, linguistic *apartheid* is applied even to juvenile gangs; these are described as composed of *ducktails* if white, of *skollys* if "colored," of *tsotsies* if black.

The doctrine of *apartheid* has its roots in South African history. When the first Dutch and French Huguenot settlers arrived in the middle of the seventeenth century, they found themselves under the despotic rule of the Dutch East India Company, which was not broken until the end of the eighteenth century. Many of them escaped it by trekking north into the then uncharted wilds. Here they encountered other invaders from beyond the Zambesi, the ancestors of the present-day Zulu-Xhosa, Bechuana-Basuto, and Ova-Herero groups, who were exterminating the aboriginal Hottentot-Bushman groups as they drove south. Armed conflict between the white and black invaders was frequent and bloody. Back in the Capetown area, meanwhile, the Dutch East

India Company countenanced a system of slavery for the Hottentots that endured almost as long as our own.

The British began to take control at the end of the eighteenth century, and British settlers first appeared in South Africa in considerable numbers in 1820. The liberal views of the British in the matter of racial equality are said to have been one of the chief reasons for the Great Trek of the Boers into the unsettled regions of the north, the founding of the Orange Free State, and the ultimate clash between Oom Paul Kruger and Cecil Rhodes that led to the Boer War.

§   §   §

New Zealand and Australia go largely together, but with a few interesting differences, partly due to the background languages of the aborigines (Polynesian-speaking Maori in New Zealand, Blackfellows with at least a hundred imperfectly known tongues in Australia). For the rest, both varieties go back in great part to London Cockney, but with plenty of individuality and creativity. Some linguists go so far as to say that Australian English is as far removed from British as is American English, but this is probably an exaggeration, in view of the strong imperial ties that were fully operative until quite recently.

In certain features of pronunciation New Zealand English comes closer to American than do either British or Australian (*dance, path,* with the *a* of *bat* rather than of *father,* is perhaps due to the fact that both countries have retained the older British pronunciation); others are individualistic (*citee, likelee, eeleven, toll* with short *o, utt uzz* for "it is"). There is also some tendency to use American rather than British word choice (*radio, pack of cigarettes, to mail,* in preference to *wireless, packet, to post*). Many vocabulary localisms coincide with those of Australia (*graft* for work, *crook* for ill, *smoko* for midmorning tea, *to chew the rag* for to brood, *bushwhacked* for tired out; but *bushed* means lost or strayed). Then there is *skite* for boast or brag, *up stick* for to move house, *be pie on* for be good at, *be on one's muttons* for be on one's guard. New Zealand prefers the French *benzine* to the English *petrol* and the American *gas*. *Sharemilker* is a sharecropper, and *squatter* means large-scale farmer. Money is sometimes referred to as *hoot*, and a recent English immigrant is a *Homey*. *Native* is the term rather precisely applied to a Maori, but while it seems harmless, it is resented by the Maori, probably by reason of connotations with which it was surrounded in the past. The Polynesian-speaking Maori have contributed *kapai*, an expression of general approval, *tenakoe* for hello, *paheka* for stranger, *rangitira* for big chief, *kia ora!* for good luck!, *mana* for prestige, and *kiwi*, the name of a wingless bird, for a doughboy. It is possible that *whare*, hut, is also a Maori loan word. Among the many terms shared with Australia are *bosker*, *dinkum*, *cobber*, *wowser*, *cow*, which will be defined later.

The settlement of New Zealand goes back to around 1840, at which time the total number of white New Zealanders was estimated at two thousand. The islands, at first annexed to Australia, were made self-governing in 1852. By 1861 there were still only about one hundred thousand whites, mostly of British birth or descent, as against over fifty thousand Maori. They were mostly sheep farmers, and it was at that time that the term *squatter* in the sense of land-rich farmer originated. In 1853 gold was discovered, and the squatters were joined by numerous *Diggers*, a term still currently used to include both New Zealanders and Australians. At the turn of the century, the white population of the islands was still below one million. Today, with new accretions from all parts of Europe, New Zealand's white English-speaking population runs well in excess of two and a half million, while the Maori have had a more modest increase to about one hundred thousand.

§   §   §

Australian English is so picturesque and replete with unique features of pronunciation and vocabulary that it has drawn numberless commentaries of varying length from both

British and American observers, as well as the more specialized attention of linguists, and particularly of the Australian Language Centre of the University of Sydney, which carries on thoroughgoing research into the history and nature of Australian English.

Here again, settlement by English speakers is recent. In 1788, after several trips of exploration, a penal colony was set up in what is today New South Wales to drain the dregs of English jails, particularly those of London, which in part accounts for the Cockney features of Australian. By 1821, the young colony numbered some thirty thousand, fully three fourths of whom were former convicts. But rehabilitation followed quickly. By 1851, when gold was discovered and people began flocking to the Australian gold fields from all countries in the world, including even America and China, there were estimated to be perhaps three hundred thousand whites, of whom some were the descendants of the original convicts, but many more were ordinary settlers from England. Most of them had gone into sheep raising in a big way. Today, the white population of Australia, drawn from practically every white country in the world, numbers well over eleven million. Nearly all of them have learned to communicate in Australian English. The aborigines are probably no more than one hundred thousand.

The phonology of Australian English is such as to have given rise to a great deal of discussion, both on the scientific and the popular plane. Eric Partridge tentatively advances the theory that the high pitch of Australian may be due not so much to Cockney ancestry as to the climate. But when placed in relation to other features (the universal long *i* for long *a*, as in *My Fair Lidy* prior to the metamorphosis), it is difficult to agree with him. There is a joke to the effect that a consumptive American who had come to Australia was asked: "Did you come here today?" He replied: "No, I came here to get well; but how did you know I was ill?"

This phonological characteristic affects what is known as Educated or Cultivated Australian as well as General and

Broad Australian, the tongues of the multitudes. The Australian Language Centre has conducted exhaustive surveys into the speech habits of a wide variety of groups, and one of the findings is that Australian speech is unusually slow and rhythmically even. An Australian conductor, Charles Mackerras, claims that this quality produces a natural singing voice. Other writers have attributed this peculiarity to the Scottish ancestry of many Australians.

Another writer, David Willis, is not so flattering to what he calls "Strine" (the popular Australian pronunciation of "Australian"). He accuses the speakers of swallowing their syllables, talking without moving either lip, and running words into each other in a steady flow of laconic, nasalized sound. In token whereof he produces the following conversation sample: "Sarn's calmner nairt. Scona beer gloria sty. Mine jute still scold zephyr. Cheat was scold la snite!", with the reply: "Weller corset Saul-wye school linnermore ninx. Buttered swarm nuddite-time. Spewffle climb a treely." For which the translation runs: "Sun's coming out. It's going to be a glorious day. Mind you, it's still cold as ever. Gee, it was cold last night!" "Well, of course it's always cool in the mornings. But it's warm in the daytime. It's a beautiful climate really."

Other samples culled at random from the Strine dictionary include *baked necks* (bacon and eggs), *rise up lides* (razor blades), *airman pickle semmitch* (ham and pickle sandwich). Without questioning the authenticity of these offerings, they impress us as basically unfair to the language, like the "Mairzy doats and dozy doats and liddle lambsie divy" of the American song of a couple of decades ago, or the "Chadoon?" which some educators claim is American English for "What are you doing?" Any type of English can be twisted out of its context by phony phonetic spellings.

Far more to the point are the Australian vocabulary offerings. A long list of early-nineteenth-century ones is supplied by the University of Sydney. These include "brush" and "bushranger"; "paddock" for field and "station" for ranch; the early "currency lad" for a native-born Australian, as against "sterling lad" for an immigrant from England; and such slangy expressions as "hump the bluey" (carry the swag), "brindabella" (a mixture of rum and beer), "Darling shower" (dust storm), "tin" (money), and the well-known "jumbuck," "billabong," and "Matilda." Among later creations are "inked" (or "shikkered") for drunk, "nark" for kibitzer, "munga" for square meal, "yacker" for hard work, "spine bash" for snooze in a reclining position. The Australian counterparts of the British Teddy Boys and Mods are "bodgies" and "widgies," with "ickies" reserved for the adults of the species. "Tart" is used as a term of endearment (our slang "tart" is their "tizzy"). "To shout" is the Australian version of the Canadian "stand sam" or the American "treat." "The big scrub" or Great Outback refer to the frontier country, "Blackfellow's gift" is almost the equivalent of our Indian giver, you "bot some oscar from a cobber" in the sense that you wangle some dough from a side-kick. Various foreign nationals are known as "Nips," Dingbats, Geordies, Chows, with a Pom or Pommie of doubtful origin once reserved for newcomers from Britain, but now applied, along with Reffo, to anyone who comes from Europe. Enzedder is a New Zealander, from the first two letters, with the second pronounced zed, British fashion. A helicopter, which is an "egg-beater" to our forces, is a "flying palm tree" to Aussie fliers. "Cooee" is a call used at a distance, but may also serve as our yoo-hoo. "Cow," which Australia shares with New Zealand, is the American slang lousy. It may be a loan translation from French *vache*, similarly used. Its opposites, covering the general area of our swell, are "ding dong," "dinkum," "bonzer," "bosker," "boshter," "slap-up." In Australia you don't smooch a jane, but "smooge a sheila" (but she may also be a "cliner," "sninny," "nice bit of skirt"). Wine is either "plonk" or "sneaky Pete." An informer is a "pimp," and a hoodlum is a "larrikin," who may "stouch you with a squirt" (attack you with a gat), but a "wowser" is a stuffed shirt. If you throw in the towel, you "sky the wipe," or "drop the bundle." A "fair go" is what we might call a fair shake. "Mateship" is far more than mere friendship, and "to dob in" is to get your mate in trouble in order to save yourself.

This could go on and on. It is easy to see why Australian, more than any other English variety save British and American, attracts the attention of scientific linguist and popular writer alike.

CHAPTER THREE

A B C D E F G H I J K L M N O P Q R S T U V W X Y Z

Your Language Says More Than You Think

Some years ago on the radio a popular show was conducted by Professor Henry Lee Smith, now of the University of Buffalo. He would undertake, usually with remarkable success, to identify what regions the program's guests came from by asking them to pronounce certain words to which regional custom has given noticeable twists. He seldom made a mistake, and when he did, it was due to what he called a mixed pattern (a person born and brought up in one locality, then transplanted to another place where he would, after years of residence, give up some of his original speech features and take on those of his adopted home). This he accomplished by using a series of imaginary east-west and north-south lines, which form the boundaries between one form of expression and another. His reasoning went something like this:

This man pronounces *merry, Mary,* and *marry* in three different fashions; this places him east of the Alleghenies. He says *greasy,* not *greazy;* this puts him somewhere north of a line running between Trenton and Philadelphia. His use of *wahsh* instead of *wush* and his use of *dawg* for *dog* and *lahg* for *log* confirm this (*dawg* and *lawg* identify a second area, *dahg* and *lahg* a third). He uses the same *a* in *park* that he uses for *father,* and that eliminates most of

New England, as does his use of the same flat *a* for *ash* and *ask*. He uses the same vowel in *horse* and *hoarse,* which means that he comes from the area between Philadelphia and New York. But his *first* sounds a little like *foist,* and this eliminates Philadelphia. So I would place him within a radius of no more than thirty miles from Times Square.

After listening to other speakers, Dr. Smith, all ears, would confidently state that they were from the Tidewater section of Virginia, or the vicinity of Pittsburgh, or south-western Indiana. Occasionally he would come out with a statement like: "You sound like a man born in eastern Texas who has lived for more than ten years in or near Washington, D.C." And he would generally be right.

There was no magic about Dr. Smith's performance— only long, hard work put in on the *Linguistic Atlas of the United States* and many, many native speakers, resulting finally in a series of valid generalizations.

The man born and bred east of the Alleghenies, whether north or south, generally avoids pronouncing his final *-r,* while the Midwesterner and Westerner usually pronounce it very distinctly and audibly, sometimes almost painfully so. The same goes for an *r* before a consonant inside a word (*father* and *farther,* for instance, will sound pretty much like *fahthuh* in eastern speech). The Easterner will give the same pronunciation to *horse* and *hoarse, for* and *four,* while the Westerner will use for *hoarse* and *four* the vowel sound of *so. Wush* or *wursh* for *wash, darter* for *daughter, paw* and *maw* for *pa* and *ma,* belong to the Midwest. The Southerner will tend to say *aig* for *egg, fin'* for *find, kep'* for *kept, chile* for *child.* The New Englander outside the Boston area will *park* his *car* with the *a* of *bat* and no audible *r,* but the Bostonese will use in *ask* and *bath* practically the same *a* he uses in *father.* A large part of the Ohio Valley will say what amounts to *beyit* for *beat,* and even *giyit* for *get.* The typical New Yorker may or may not say *boid* for *bird* and *erl* for *oil,* but unless he is educated out of it he will replace the *th* of *three* with *t,* and the *th* of *this* with *d.* He will pronounce *wetting* and *wedding* the same way and use *bo'uhl* for *bottle*. He will use the same *ng* in *singer* that he uses in *finger*, and if the *ng* comes at the end of a word and the next word starts with a vowel, he will carry the *g* over (*gettin gout* for *getting out*). The *ou* of *about the house* will sound peculiar in the mouth of either a Virginian or a Canadian, but the Virginian will surround it with Southern features and drop his final *-r*, the Canadian will talk like a Midwesterner and pronounce his *-r*.

Not only in the way they pronounce words but also in their choice and combination of words, people reveal their origins. What an Easterner calls a paper "bag" a Midwesterner would call a paper "sack," and a Southerner might easily call a paper "poke." What many people call a Coke might be a "tonic" in parts of New England, a "soft drink" in many parts of the nation, a "dope" in parts of the South. Anyone who calls a green pepper a "mango" is almost certainly from the Midwest, most probably from Ohio. If a large sandwich is called a "hoagy," a "hero," or a "poorboy," it would be a clue that the speaker is respectively from Philadelphia, New York, or the South. "You bet" used for "You're welcome" or "Don't mention it" identifies a speaker generally as a Midwesterner, particularly from the Chicago area. Philadelphians say "square" and "pavement" for what others call "city block" and "sidewalk." Where most people "park" cars, residents of Trenton "rank" them, and those of southern Delaware "file" them.

These differences, while purely local, are still fairly legitimate English. Beyond them are out-and-out dialects and slang usages that take liberties with the English language. "Get shut of" for get rid of and "jin" for do hard work are characteristic of the Ohio Valley. "Cabbage onto" for get hold of would identify a native of Oklahoma, and "I don't belong to get up till nine a.m.," a native of Idaho. Southern girls are sometimes "carried," rather than taken, to dances. The Pennsylvania Dutch have contributed such speech mannerisms as "the milk is all [gone]," "outen [put out] the light," and "the paper wants [predicts] rain." If the speaker uses "youse" in addressing a plural audience, he is likely to be from the New York area; if he says "you-all," he is more likely to be from the South; "you-uns," and even an occasional "us-uns" for we marks him as coming from the mountain region of the Appalachian divide.

§   §   §

Foreign accents definitely offer clues as to the national origin of the speaker. In fact, they are so numerous and outstanding that they used to lend themselves well to vaudeville comedy. An audience that knows no French, no Italian, no Yiddish, will nevertheless laugh at the comedian who impersonates one of those groups, largely by his assumed accent.

The linguistic fact is that anyone learning another language at the adult stage carries over into his newly acquired tongue many of the sounds and speech habits of his original language. These he will use as substitutes for those sounds and processes that he finds difficult. The American learning French, for instance, will tend to substitute his own American cupped *r* for the gently rasping throat *r* that is characteristic of good Parisian. In like manner, the Frenchman learning English will be almost certain to carry over his *r*-sound, which is like a gentle clearing of the throat ("uvular *r*" is its phonetic name, because it is produced by letting the air issuing from the windpipe vibrate against the uvula in the back of the throat). The Frenchman is normally unable or unwilling to produce our two *th*-sounds; he will substitute for them, most frequently, an *s* and a *z*, thus producing the sort of thing that is lampooned in the comic strips as *zees seeng* for *this thing*. But the thing that most characterizes the Frenchman trying to speak English is his distributing the stress evenly over a word of two or more syllables. To an English speaker, who usually stresses the beginning of the word, this sounds as though the Frenchman were putting his stress on the ending, and pronouncing the other unstressed syllables of the word far more distinctly than we do. A comic strip might lampoon the Frenchman's pronunciation of *interesting* as *een-tayr-est*-EENG.

A German speaker, particularly if he is from the mountain regions of southern Germany, Austria, or Switzerland, tends to pronounce *st-, sp-* at the beginning of a word as *sht-, shp-*. In a British film depicting the creation of the famous World War II fighter plane, the German pilots nearing the English coast give warning to one another of the approach of enemy planes by calling out "SHPIT-fire!" The German speaker also tends to pronounce our final *-d, -g, -b, -v* sounds as *-t, -k, -p, -f*, since his own language does not permit voiced consonants in the final position (in German you write *und der Tag*, but you pronounce *unt der Tak*). The vowels which the English speaker pronounces with a glide (like the *o* of *so*) will have no glide in the mouth of a German speaker, so you will hear him pronounce *so* as *soh*, or possibly *zoh*, because many German speakers pronounce an initial *s-* as *z-*. An initial *w-* will usually come out as *v-* (*vell* for *well*). In extreme cases, if the German speaker's knowledge of English is very sketchy, he may unconsciously use a few common German words in replacement of their English equivalents (*oder* for *or, mit* for *with*). *Zoh I vill giff you a goot shlice uf bret mit cheess* may be a comic strip rendering of the speech of Mrs. Katzenjammer, but it may also be the way a German who has learned English imperfectly actually speaks.

A native Spanish speaker can usually be identified by the fact that he gives his initial *h-* in English a much rougher, more rasping sound than English speakers do (*khat* for *hat*); this is because he is using the sound of Spanish *j* in substitution for our *h*-sound, which Castilian Spanish lacks. Even more general and outstanding is the Spanish speaker's tendency to put a vowel sound (something like the *e* of *the*) in front of any initial *st-, sp-, str-, spr-* (this is because in Spanish no word ever begins with those consonant combinations; our special is their *especial,* our state their *estado,* etc.). In common with the Italian speaker (who has no trouble at all with our *st-, sp-*), the Spanish speaker finds it difficult to distinguish between the vowel sound of *live* and that of *leave,* or *hull* and *hall,* and tends to interchange them (*I leave in New York; I live for Puerto Rico tomorrow*).

The Italian speaker often has trouble with final consonant groups, and tends to put an echo vowel after them, so that *Pittsburgh* sounds like *Pittsburgher* (as pronounced by an Easterner, without final *-r*), and *Buick* sounds like BOO-*ee-kuh.* The Italian speaker has trouble with his *th*-sounds, which the Spanish speaker does not; the Italian may say *dees ting* for *this thing.*

A native speaker of Russian tends to put a *y*-glide in front of an *i*-sound, so that *any* sounds like *a-nyi,* and *pity* like *pyi-tyi.* He will often turn our short *i* inside a word into a sound pronounced far back in the mouth, so that *wing* will have the vowel sound of *rhythm.* Like the German, he will pronounce our final *-d, -b, -g, -v* sounds as *-t, -p, -k, -f.*

The Hungarian speaker's English will be slow, deliberate, over-clear, with very precise enunciation. The Czech will use a staccato pronunciation that faintly reminds you of the rattle of a machine gun. A Russian, Czech, or Pole will often leave out the words *the, a,* or *an,* which do not appear in their languages, and say "I put book on table" for " I put a book on the table." Scandinavian speakers, particularly Swedes and Norwegians, have a singsong lilt in their voices, which go up and down with what amounts to a musical cadence. Both have trouble with the sound of *j,* or of *g* in words like *gentle,* and tend to replace it with *y* (*yoin* for *join, yentle* for *gentle*).

A Greek speaker can usually be told by his sharp, hissing *s,* combined with the fact that he has absolutely no difficulty with our *th*-sounds, which appear plentifully in his language. It is generally possible to distinguish between a Chinese and a Japanese speaker by the fact that the Chinese replaces our *r* with *l* (*flied lice* for *fried rice*), while the Japanese replaces our *l* with a lightly trilled *r* (*I rike you* for *I like you*).

§   §   §

There is also an entire technique for determining from a person's written language what his place of origin may be. Here the clues involve the general handwriting, size and type of letters, flourishes, use of capitals and punctuation, significant misspellings, use of certain words, expressions, and grammatical arrangement. As described in an earlier chapter, the spelling *honour* for *honor* would mark the writer as non-American. An American would not normally cross his figure seven; most continental Europeans do. Capitalizing common nouns in English would constitute *prima facie* evidence of the writer's German nationality.

Detective work on the written word is no mere fiction. Like verbal detection, it has its own long history. In sixteenth-century France, largely as a result of the Protestant Reformation, many lawsuits sought to deprive the established Catholic Church of some of its lands. The Catholics' claims to ownership generally rested on deeds that had been written seven or eight centuries earlier. The authenticity of these documents was now questioned by the reform forces. They were forgeries, the Protestants claimed, that had been composed centuries after they were supposed to have been written. At this point, language detectives were called in to settle the disputes. If the experts found that eighth-century kings had deeded lands in language that did not come into use until the twelfth century, the verdict would be forgery.

A prize case of language detection is that of the Rosetta stone, discovered in Egypt in Napoleon's time. The stone bore what appeared to be the identical inscription in three forms: Egyptian hieroglyphic and Egyptian demotic, as yet undeciphered, and Greek, which was known. The trick was to figure out the ancient Egyptian languages from the Greek. Royal names were known to be enclosed in *cartouches,* or ellipses. The Greek inscription bore the names of Ptolemy and Cleopatra; the Egyptian *cartouches,* then, must also hold these names. Thus a certain Egyptian symbol must stand for *p,* another for *t, l, m,* and so forth. This was the first clue to the dead Egyptian language. It took many years to figure out the whole passage on the stone, but as clue piled on clue, the work was finally completed. Today, as a result of the pioneering work on the Rosetta stone, an Egyptologist can read most of the ancient language with comparative ease.

Non-Egyptologists—in fact, people with only a smattering of linguistic knowledge—can find language detective work useful in day-to-day living, in such cases as determining a person's nationality from the spelling of his name. *Van,* for instance, is Dutch, and *von* is German. *Mc* is Irish, and *Mac* Scottish. An *-ez* ending is Spanish, an *-ov* or *-off* ending Russian, an *-i* usually Italian. Names that end in *-quist, -rup,* and *-holm* are Scandinavian; those ending in *-escu* are Rumanian, in *-wicz* Polish, *-en* Finnish, *-ian* Armenian, *-oglu* Turkish, and *-poulos* Greek. Though originally foreign, names too contribute to the variety of American English.

Pidgin English Around the World

George Bernard Shaw has Androcles address the Lion in this fashion: "Did um get um awful thorn in um's tootsums wootsums?"

This type of speech, called hypocorism by the scientists and baby talk by the layman, differs in degree but not in kind from the first impression of New York voiced by a Solomon Islands chieftain on a visit here: "Me lookum one big fella place. He high up too much. He alla same one fella mountain."

Hypocorism is what we perpetrate on our young children, who without it would grow up speaking as good English as their elders. Noah Webster, earliest American authority on the subject, said: "The silly language called baby talk, in which most persons are initiated in infancy, often breaks out in discourse at the age of forty, and makes a man appear very ridiculous. A boy of six years may be taught to speak as correctly as Cicero did before the Roman Senate."

Pidgin, the adult, international, and interracial version of hypocorism, is what we have done to those adult children who first began to be the "white man's burden" in the seventeenth century—the natives of the trade ports of China, the islands of the Pacific, the west coast of Africa, and many other far-flung localities.

In Hong Kong your ear will be caught by "chop-chop" (quickly) and "numba one first chop" (superfine); "all-same," "blongee," "catchee" (to have), "dlinkee," and such picturesque combinations as "have got wata top side" (crazy). An Englishman used to be known as "Ah say," from the English custom of interjecting "I say!" into the conversation, and a Portuguese was similarly known as "ah kee" (Portuguese *aqui,* here).

In the Solomons and New Guinea it is "put clothes belong table" (set the table) and "cut 'im grass belong head belong me" (cut my hair); "water he kai-kai 'im" (he drowned) and "man belong bullamacow 'im stop" (the butcher is here). In Samoa it's "apple belong stink" (onion) and " 'im fella coconut 'im bad" (he has a headache). In Hawaii a radio performer says to her announcer "you regla popoki awaawa dis morning!" meaning he's a sourpuss. And in West Africa you hear "Who dat man?" (who goes there?) and "one-time" (hurry up). All this, outside of a few loan words from the native languages (*kai-kai, popoki awaawa*), is English; quite different from the English spoken in New York or London, but English nevertheless, in much the same fashion that "dadums," "momsie," "woofies," and "bekus puddy" are English.

The number of pidgin English speakers throughout the world is estimated at between thirty and fifty million, which is greater than the number of speakers of Dutch, Czech, Swedish, or Hungarian; in fact, of all but a handful of the world's major tongues. Pidgin is neither a dead nor a dying language. The Hobart (Tasmania) *Mercury* some time ago stressed the fact that pidgin is the only means of communication with the natives in certain quite extensive areas. The director of education in Lagos, on the West African coast, says: "In several polyglot areas Pidgin is the only possible medium in the lowest forms of our elementary schools." The West Pacific high commissioner of Suva, in the Fiji Islands, says: "I am convinced it is a living language which is expanding rapidly and with increasing vitality." During the

Second World War the Japanese found it not merely expedient, but necessary to issue millions of propaganda pamphlets in pidgin, and the Americans, British, and Australians took up the practice as they reconquered the islands. In New Guinea, since 1935, a monthly magazine entitled *Frend Belong Mi* has been published by Catholic missionaries; it is completely composed in pidgin, even to the fiction and crossword puzzles.

§   §   §

The history of pidgin is a simple one. It began in the trade ports of South China, where some means of common intercourse had to be devised between the Chinese and the Western traders (the word "pidgin" itself is the Cantonese corruption of the English business, so that "Pidgin English" is really business English; an apprentice today is still called "larn-pidgin"). The compromise lay along the line of least resistance, which consisted for the most part of using English words with Chinese word arrangement and syntax. This meant using such expressions as "cow-child" for girl and "bull-child" for boy, disregarding factors of number and gender, making the verbs timeless and invariable, and using translations of Chinese classifiers ("fella" in connection with any human being, as in "one fella Mary," meaning a woman, and "piecee" in connection with inanimate objects, as in "two piecee shirt" for two shirts). It might have been almost equally easy to teach the Chinese straight English; but the traders thought the Chinese would learn faster if their pattern of thought and speech was respected in the translation of words.

Spreading southward, the pidgin habit progressed to the Pacific islands, where it turned into the pidgin *par excellence,* Melanesian Pidgin English. This was taken up not only by the copra traders and growers but also by missionaries, and religious instruction was imparted in the new medium. Then it moved on to Australia, New Guinea, Samoa, and Hawaii.

But the variety current in the Melanesian Islands (Solomons, Fiji, New Hebrides, etc.) is the most widespread. This linguistic form, which in some localities has become fully standardized, and has even been reduced to rules of phonology, grammar, and syntax, shows forms at least as picturesque as those of China. "Me like" is "I want"; "Kiss 'im soo-soo, ee come" is "Bring me some milk"; "By 'n' by me buy 'im long how mas mark?" is the inquiry "How much?" Yes is commonly expressed by "ee got," No by "no got." For "What is your name?" the formula is "Call 'im name belong you." "It's very far" sounds like teen-age talk: "Man, ee go go go go." For hotel, rest room, dwelling house, use "house drink," "house peck peck," "house married," respectively. Boy is "monkey," and girl is "monkey Mary." Bad, reasonably enough, is "no good," like Esperanto *malbona.*

Pidgin is spoken slowly, emphatically, even majestically, and in a very loud voice. Also, regrettably, it is chock-full of profanity and obscenity. This, of course, is the heritage of the traders and soldiers, not at all of the missionaries, who steadfastly but vainly strive to eradicate it. An American officer stationed in the Solomons reported that on one occasion a native chieftain observed with growing astonishment the vast quantities of supplies that came off the American ships. Finally he could stand it no longer. "Mission fella man" he remarked to the officer, "'im 'e say God make everything. Bullshit! America make everything!" But most pidgin speakers, proud of their recently won Christianity, aver: "Me belong Big Fella along top!"

The white man adapts himself rather well to pidgin. Consider, for instance, the terse directness of this address, made to the natives by a physician sent by the Rockefeller Foundation to the Melanesian Islands to eradicate the hookworm:

"Master belong me, 'im make 'im altogether kerosene, 'im make 'im altogether benzine. Now he old fella. He got 'im plenty too much belong money. Money belong 'im allasame dirt. Now he old fella, close up 'im he die finish. He look about. 'Im he think, 'Me like make 'im one fella something, he good fella belong altogether boy he buy 'im kerosene belong me.' Master belong me 'im he talk, 'You, you go kill 'im altogether snake belong belly belong boy belong island!' "

Or, to take another sample, here is the account of the wedding of Queen Elizabeth that appeared at Lae in New Guinea:

"Good news 'e come up along England. Long Friday twentieth November, number one piccininni belong king belong you and me, King George VI long England, 'e marry. Now 'im 'e got two piccininni, Misses Princess Elizabeth now Princess Margaret Rose. Now Princess Elizabeth 'im 'e got marry long one fella man name belong Duke Edinburgh. All 'e hurrah much long this fella princess."

Imagery, both profane and poetic, abounds in pidgin. A piano is "Hit 'im in teeth, out come squeal allasame pig" and a violin is "scratch 'im in belly, out come squeak allasame pussycat." An intellectual is "think fella too much." An automobile is "eat 'im wind cart," and a train "big fella firesnake."

Other interesting samples come from New Guinea. "Capsize 'im coffee along cup" (pour the coffee); "New fella moon 'e come up" (it's the first of the month); "Skin belong you 'im stink (you need a bath); "Make 'im die machine" (stop the engine); "Two clock he go finish, three clock 'e no come up yet" (it's half past two); "Shoot 'im kai-kai" (serve the dinner); "Me cross too much along you" (I'm very angry with you).

A characteristic process of pidgin is that of repetition to express intensity or thoroughness. "You go go go" (keep on going); "bamboo belong look-look" (spyglass); "wash wash" (to bathe, in contradistinction to mere wash); "talk-talk" (long palaver, as against mere talk). This is reminiscent of what goes on in many more cultured tongues, like the Italian *piano piano,* very softly.

Other curious parallels appear: "me-fella," "you-fella," "'em-all" (respectively for "we," plural "you," "they," like

Southern you-all). "How much clock?" for "What time is it?" reminds one of German, from which it may well have been borrowed, for Germany had extensive Pacific possessions before the First World War. The pidgin use of "belly" to denote the seat of the emotions coincides with the ancient Greek belief that the stomach was the place where the emotions were born and bred. The use of "bone" to denote courage ("'Im got plenty bone"), or the lack of courage ("Bone belong 'im allasame water," meaning that he's scared to death) has a curious similarity to our own use of "backbone" and "spineless," and perhaps even to our "tough."

The islands have received contributions to their pidgin English from non-English sources. A Frenchman is variously known as "man-a-wi-wi," man of *oui, oui;* "montour" (*bonjour*), "montwar" (*bonsoir*); in Java, he is known as "orang deedong," *orang* being Malay for man, while *deedong* is French *dites donc.* Local variations of pidgin include such different forms as *kai-kai, chow-chow, kau-kau, fu-fu,* used on different islands in the sense of to eat.

The Australian Blackfellows use a variety of pidgin that largely coincides with the Melanesian and New Guinea brands, but sometimes contributes its own special expressions: "paper-yabber along big fella hawk" (airmail); "kill 'im stink fella" (disinfectant).

Bèche la Mer, or Sandalwood English, is the form taken by pidgin in the southern islands of Polynesia (Samoa, Tahiti, etc.). The addition of -*um* to verbs is characteristic ("eatum," "callum," "catchum"). So are "water belong stink" (perfume) and "belly belong me walk about too much" (I have a stomach-ache).

Hawaii supplies us with what may be described as our own American variety of pidgin. The Hawaiian language does not permit two consonants to follow each other, or a consonant to appear at the end of a word. Furthermore, many consonants, including *b, d, f, g, j, r, s, t, v,* do not appear in the language. The result is that when a Hawaiian who has not had school training attempts to say "Merry

Christmas!" he comes out with "Mele Kalikimaka!" The names of the months, all borrowed from English, take the following forms in Hawaiian: *Ianuali, Pepeluali, Malaki, Apelila, Mei, Iune, Iulae, Aukake, Kemakemapa, Okakopa, Nowemapa, Kekemapa.* Many native words and expressions have crept into the English of residents from the American continent, and thence back to America itself: *wahini* (woman), *no* (yes), *malihini* (stranger), and, of course, *lei, luau, hukilau,* and *aloha oe,* which is both hello and good-bye.

§   §   §

It is uncertain whether the West African variety of pidgin was derived from or influenced by the Pacific branch. The nature of pidgin is such that it could well have arisen independently in separate parts of the globe. In West African pidgin there are such terms as "no humbug me," "wait small" (wait a while), "jagwah" (this was originally Jaguar, but is applied to any car). "Been-to" is an African who has been to Britain, and if educated he becomes "megotbuk" or even "megotbukbuk." If he owns a car or a refrigerator, he turns into a "carful" or "fridgeful." "He threw a vex," and "This is not for pleasuring" are specifically Liberian. Official status has finally been achieved by West African pidgin in the form of Krio, a compromise of English, French, Portuguese, and at least seventeen native languages, now semi-official in some West African states and said to be spoken by at least twenty-five thousand people.

There are several forms of bastardized English that are definitely known to have no connection with the main pidgin stock. There are, for instance, the American Indian forms used upon our own aborigines in the days of coloniza-tion. "How?", "paleface," "heap big chief," "firewater," "plentum," interspersed with authentic native words like *squaw, papoose, wampum, wigwam, moccasin,* are fair samples of this pidgin language which died a-borning. One of its most extensive varieties was the Chinook jargon of the Northwest, which contained French elements contributed by the French Canadians, such as *lelang* and *leman* (*la langue* and *la main*).

The Ningre-Tongo or Talkie-Talkie of Dutch Guiana, the Kitchen Kaffir of South Africa, the Afro-American Gullah of South Carolina all prove that English can be pidginized in separate and unrelated corners of the earth. The English of Jamaica can be altogether correct, as evidenced by the famous calypsos, but it can also show such unfamiliar forms as "freeness" (for liberality), "don't worry with me," and names of steel-band instruments like the "tock-tock," "shac-shac," "boom," and "ping-pong."

A measure of topical interest attaches to the pidgin of India, by reason of the fact that India claims to be the third greatest English-speaking nation on earth, with perhaps twenty-five million English speakers in a country of well over four hundred million. If Hindi ever becomes the sole official tongue of India, these English speakers will nevertheless continue to flourish in their evil ways, as typified by the *babu*, or scribe, who wrote to complain that he had found himself "suddenly disemployed," although he had to support a family consisting of "four adults and three adulteresses." Other choice samples of Anglo-Indian are "this-all," "a fun," "to marry with," "as if" (this, all by itself, is an expression of indignant surprise), "cousin mother" (for aunt), "isn't it?" (used exactly like French *n'est-ce pas?* or German *nicht wahr?*).

Anglo-Indian pidgin is also known as Hobson-Jobson, a name that comes from the Moslem rallying-cry, "Ya, Hassan! Ya, Hussein!", frequently heard in the old communal wars between Moslems and Hindus, Hassan and Hussein being two Moslem saints. In the older variety of Anglo-Indian, a *bahadur* was a stuffed shirt, and there were verbs like *to dumbcow* (meaning to browbeat, derived from Hindi *dumkhānā*, to eat one's breath); *to foozilow* (flatter); *to puckerow* (lay hold of). *Summer heat* for hat came from Spanish *sombrero*, with a little imaginative crossing; *goddess* for girl was the Malay *gādīs*; and the graphic expression for cholera, *mort-de-chien*, looked like French for *a dog's death*, but actually came from Marathi *modwashī*.

Many words entered standard English from Hobson-Jobson: *betel, mango, curry, cheroot, bungalow, pariah, tiffin*, and *griffin* (the last meant a newcomer). A colloquialism like *grass widow* arose in India, where British officers' wives were sent to the cool, grassy hills, while their husbands sweltered in the hot, dusty plains. The slangy *cheese* of *big cheese* is the Hindi *chīz*, thing, and the *damn* of "I don't give a damn" is the Hindi *dām*, a small coin. Among more recent additions to English from this source are *coggage* (papers, documents); *tiggerty-boo,* which for a time rivalled O.K., came from Hindi *tīga,* and is said to have been first introduced to England by Lord Louis Mountbatten.

Indonesia and other Asian regions contribute such forms as "incharge" for the man who is in charge, "wears and tears," "newses," and "can" in the sense of "yes."

§   §   §

There are not only numerous varieties of pidgin English, but also pidgins of other tongues. The most important of these is pidgin Malay—which the Dutch used to call *pasar* (or *bazaar*) *Malay*—a compromise of various Malayo-Polynesian dialects that extended throughout the Malay Peninsula and the former Dutch East Indies, and was understood as far as the Philippines. It was this Malay that supplied the base for one of the world's most recent national languages, Indonesian.

A *Petit-Nègre*, or French pidgin, appears in French West Africa, side by side with West African pidgin English. Several forms of Portuguese pidgin are in existence, both on the West African coast and in some cities of India. A Tagalog-Spanish pidgin appears in the Philippines. Papiamento is a picturesque Spanish-Portuguese pidgin used by the native population in Curaçao, in the Dutch West Indies. The French Creole of Haiti and Louisiana, the

Dutch Creole of Georgetown and the Virgin Islands, and the Portuguese Creole of the Cape Verde Islands, are all forms of pidgin.

In much earlier times the lingua franca of the Mediterranean—a pidginized form of Italian crossed with elements taken from French, Greek, and Arabic—was widely used by medieval and Renaissance traders and sailors. Before that came the literary Franco-Venetian of the thirteenth-century *jongleurs,* who devised a linguistic compromise between French and Italian so that they could bring the rich tradition of the French *chansons de geste* to the avid ears of Italian audiences.

The question is sometimes raised whether immigrant dialects should be viewed as pidgins. They, too, represent a blend of the language of the country of origin with that of the country to which the emigrants have gone. Some are quite elaborate. This is true of the Cocoliche of Buenos Aires, which is an almost perfect blend of Spanish and Italian, two languages that mix rather easily; as well as of the Pochismo ("discolored language") of the United States-Mexican border, which gives us such expressions as *jatqueque* (hot cake), *te y ponque* (tea and pound cake), *lleñeral* (ginger ale), and even *jamachi* (how much?). There is the Italian immigrant dialect represented by such typical formations as *lotti* and *plotti* (lots and plots; national Italian would render these as *appezzamenti di terreno*), *grosseria* (grocery; the proper Italian term is *pizzicheria*), and even *ghenga di loffari* (gang of loafers; properly rendered by *banda di fannulloni*) and *sanamagogna* (son-of-a-gun). The distinguishing mark seems to be the instability and evanescence of the immigrant dialect, which disappears in a couple of generations, as compared with the hardy vitality and continued use of the pidgin.

One would be tempted on this basis to describe as a pidgin the Pennsylvania "Dutch" of York and Lancaster counties, which is not at all Dutch, but a blend of English and High German. The speakers of Pennsylvania German originally came from the Palatinate, and the naming error goes back to our own misuse of "Dutch," which comes from *Deutsch,* but which we apply to Hollanders, who never use it. Some of the speakers of Pennsylvania German take the language quite seriously, to the extent of establishing courses in it at Muhlenberg College in Allentown, Pennsylvania. Others treat it as a spoof, as indicated by the following samples which may, however, be authentic enough: "He's on his off (vacation), but his off is almost all" (finished); "The farm was daughtered off" (passed on to sons-in-law); "Bump, the button don't bell" (Knock, the bell doesn't ring); "Jakie went to town mit himself alone"; "Come from the woodpile in; mom's on the table, and pop he et himself done already"; "What for kind of thing is that, it makes so funny?"; "Aunt Emmy's wonderful sick; she don't feel so pretty good."

§   §   §

Two facts stand out significantly in connection with pidgin. The first is that, far from dying out, it seems to be expanding with abundant vitality. The other is that English seems to lend itself to pidginization more than any other tongue. This causes one to wonder whether there may not be a projection of pidgin into the future.

Shorn of its picturesque and humorous features, what does pidgin portend? Does it perhaps point to the shape of things to come, an international language of the future that may eventually do service for universal linguistic exchange, if the world's governments do not forestall it in time by selecting an official world tongue?

Pidgin is indeed a symbol of man's erroneous and inefficient thinking. But it is also a monument to human ingenuity. It displays the multiplicity of wrong roads the human mind can take, but also the relentless will of man to create understanding under the most difficult of circumstances. When Argentina creates a common tongue of intercourse like Cocoliche out of two related tongues like Spanish and Italian, it is not very surprising. But when the faraway corners of the earth produce a meeting ground of understanding out of languages with no common origin or base, such as Chinese and English, Melanesian and English, West African and English, there is occasion to marvel. Does the phenomenon perhaps indicate that human beings, left to their own devices and freed from artificial, government-inspired propaganda (even if the latter is disguised as a plea for linguistic and cultural purity), would seek and find comprehension and, eventually, tolerance? The implications are best left to the sociologist.

It remains for the linguist to explain why English, more than any other language, has developed pidgin forms. The reason lies in part, but only in part, in the greater aggressiveness in navigation and colonization of the English-speaking peoples. Actually, one must remember that seafaring and colonization were far from being the exclusive prerogative of English speakers in the sixteenth, seventeenth, and eighteenth centuries. French, Dutch, Portuguese, and Spaniards did as much as the English in the way of discovery, exploration, navigation, and trading. Yet the pidgin forms to which their languages gave rise are scanty in number and geographical extent as compared with the imposing mass of pidgin English.

The real fact of the matter seems to be that among all Western languages, English most readily lends itself to pidginization—that is, to the simplification and distortion that make the language accessible to foreign groups without at the same time removing it from the comprehension of its own native speakers.

In part, this is because English has already reduced flectional endings, verb forms, and complications of gender, number, and case to a minimum. If one is compelled by reason of ignorance to forgo grammatical and syntactical correctness and literary expression, he can nevertheless make himself understood in English by a mere use of vocabulary. This is hardly true of the other great Western languages.

A comparison between pidgin English and the pidgin French of Louisiana or Haiti makes this quite evident. An English speaker can get the gist of a pidgin English passage, but a French speaker needs special instruction to understand pidgin French, where the abolition of endings results in virtual breakdown of understanding.

The willingness of English to grant naturalization to foreign words also plays a part. All languages accept borrowed words from other tongues, but no other great Western language does so to the same astounding degree as our own. This means that the primitive group that chooses, in a pidgin English pattern, to insert its own distinctive words, like the *kai-kai* and *kinkenau* of the Melanesians, may do so, and have its choice respected and quietly accepted by the English speakers with whom it comes in contact. English has adhered to this process of linguistic liberalism since its very inception, when Anglo-Saxon borrowed words like *street, cheese, kiln,* and *minster* from Latin; *bishop, church,* and *angel* from Greek; *they, knife, husband,* and *ugly* from Scandinavian; *bald, crag, crock,* and *bard* from Celtic.

Much has been said in recent times of Basic English and its paraphrasing process, whereby a limited number of words, by a method of constant repetition and ingenious combination, is made to do the work of a much larger vocabulary. The analogy with pidgin is striking. In pidgin, too, a word like "belong" does service for "of," the possessive case, and a vast number of other intricate constructions.

Basic, however, goes no farther than to attempt to simplify the process of vocabulary learning so as to ensure acceptance of English by foreign speakers. Pidgin, on the other hand, points to what is possibly an additional, though unspoken, desire on the part of foreign speakers—a desire for further simplification of English grammar and syntax, something that will remove the stumbling block presented by such verb forms as *see, saw, seen,* irregular plurals like *oxen, mice, children,* complex subordinate clauses and prepositional phrases. Perhaps what is needed is some system of "model English," offering an invariable present tense always in the infinitive form ("I be," "he be," instead of I am, he is), a past tense invariably formed with *did* ("I did see" for I saw), and plurals that are always regular ("childs" and "deers" for children and deer).

Whether such deliberate pidginization of English would be worth while, whether it would prove acceptable, whether it would not arouse competition of a similar nature from other languages, is something that would have to be carefully studied.

In the meantime, pidgin English stands as a marker of man's linguistic frailty and linguistic ambition, a living tribute to those forces within man that impel him to seek the understanding of his fellow, at any cost, and by any method available.

PART TWO

a b c d e f g h i j k l m n o p q r s t u v w x y z

THE FLUX OF
ENGLISH

THE COURSE OF THE ENGLISH LANGUAGE DOES *not run smooth. It is beset by shoals and sand banks that may not be insurmountable, but do present problems. A few are discussed in the following five chapters: What to do about our ever-growing number of words? Are all these words desirable, from whatever source they may come? To what extent does the language of commercialism interfere with the general language's natural flow? Ought we to direct our conscious thoughts to the matter of language reform, and dredge our river bed? Is standardization necessary, or even desirable, in order to assure a more even flow? Above all, what of the thorny issue of spelling reform? What are the real obstacles in its path? If we decide to solve it, should the solution be an altogether radical one, on the basis of phonetic realities, or is some sort of compromise possible?*

Have We Too Many Words?

One often hears the claim that the average man's vocabulary is extremely limited. Some years ago, a study based on the language of fruit pickers resulted in the startling conclusion that the illiterate and semi-literate among us get along with no more than 500 words. A little later, the late Max Sherover, president of the Linguaphone Institute, determined, on the basis of subway conversations, that the average person normally uses between 1,000 and 2,000 words.

These figures have been strongly disputed. Reputable psychologists have advanced the theory that the average child of four knows over 5,000 words, the boy of ten about 30,000, and the literate adult up to 60,000, or, in some cases, as many as 100,000.

Part of the discrepancy is accounted for by the distinction, carefully made by linguists, between use vocabulary and recognition vocabulary. When heard or seen, hundreds of words are understood and recognized that are not normally used in everyday conversation.

The surprising fact nevertheless remains that the maximum vocabulary of the most learned does not extend very far beyond the 100,000 mark, while the number of words appearing in the comprehensive dictionaries (the New Oxford, for instance) runs to well over 600,000. Since even the New Oxford does not include all words in use, and hundreds of new words are coined every day, this means simply that no matter how educated you manage to become, no matter how vast your cultural range, you cannot hope to master more than approximately one word out of ten *in your own language*. It would seem, therefore, that the best of us are no more than semi-literate.

Precisely the same situation holds in all other civilized tongues. Some languages are richer in words than others; but few are the languages of Western or Eastern culture whose complete vocabulary does not register at least half a million words. These vocabularies are far from static, and without exception are growing at a rapid pace. More and more words clamor for admission, while the words already in existence are extremely reluctant to drop out.

Language is, after all, but a reflection of the human race and its activity, and the experience of language duplicates that of mankind. The world's population is today at least three times what it was less than a century ago, and man's activity has become increasingly multiform. Some people die, certain practices and occupations tend to disappear. But for every individual that dies, at least two are born. For every activity that becomes obsolete, five new ones arise. Sociologists wonder what we shall do with the earth's population a century hence. Labor experts, who in the nineteenth century used to worry about every new invention and piece of machinery by reason of the unemployment they thought it would create, are preoccupied less and less on that score; rather, they wonder how modern man can possibly keep up with all the things there are for him to do. Linguists, who in the past eagerly welcomed vocabulary accretions, are at present beginning to wonder just where the growth of language is leading us.

Historically, we find that language keeps pace with the growth of civilization and the multiplication of human activities. Little-known languages, like those of the American Indians or the Australian aborigines, have more restricted vocabularies than the tongues of civilization, not because of any inherent inferiority, but simply because they do not experience to the same degree the need to name objects, qualities, and forms of activity (incidentally, for what concerns their more limited range of activities, their vocabularies and the precision of their distinctions are equal to our own). As man's civilization grows, along with his range of things, doings, and concepts, so necessarily does his vocabulary. The civilizations of classical antiquity were, from a purely material standpoint, less complex than our own. At the same time, the recorded total vocabulary of languages like Greek and Latin runs to about 100,000 words, which indicates that those civilizations were complex enough to tax, from the angle of vocabulary, the ablest type of human brain. But the recorded figures of those languages, drawn from the vocabulary of surviving literature, leave out of account many words that must have been current and that did not get into that portion of the classical writings that has come down to us, so that we are forced to conclude that those tongues, at their most flourishing period, may well have had total vocabularies of 200,000 or more words.

Medieval languages, such as Anglo-Saxon, Old French, and Old High German, display a relative poverty of words. This is in part due to the fact that many words went unrecorded in that period of widespread illiteracy, but it must also reflect the slackening of human activity, material and intellectual, that attended the downfall of the Roman Empire of the West and the settling of feudal gloom upon its lands. Even at this period, however, we are amazed at the creative power displayed by those tongues. The refined terminology of Greek and Latin authors disappears, true; but it is to a considerable extent replaced by a new religious vocabulary that reflects the spiritual interests of the medieval world.

With the Renaissance comes a new process, one that may be described as conservation of what the languages already possessed coupled with accretion from what they had once lost and now find again, as well as from their own independent creativeness. A tongue like French retains in large measure its native stock of words, consisting of Latin survivors and newcomers brought in by the Germanic invaders. To these are added myriads of words that had existed in Latin and Greek, but had been forgotten in the intervening centuries, and are now "rediscovered." Sometimes the rediscovered word is one that had in reality survived all the time, but whose identity had been disguised. Latin *fragilis,* for instance, through natural popular transformations had give rise to French *frêle,* but when the scholars of the Renaissance saw *fragilis* in Latin literary works they could not resist the temptation to reintroduce it in the form of *fragile.* English, borrowing both words from French, has *frail* and *fragile,* differing as to use and meaning, but both from the same original source.

§   §   §

Important as is the process of learned importation from the classical tongues in languages like English and French, it is still secondary to two other vocabulary-building processes: that of importation from other living tongues (as when words like *sombrero, frankfurter, hors d'oeuvre, spaghetti, taboo, wampum, boomerang* come into English); and that of creation by combining existing roots with existing prefixes and suffixes (like *intertwine* from *twine,* or *Protestantism* from *Protestant*), or with other roots, to obtain a new word descriptive of an object, quality, state of mind, or action for which a need is felt. *Railroad* is a case in point. Before the new mode of locomotion existed, we had both rails and roads, as objects and as words. The combination of the two words gave us a new name for a new object. *Carpetbagger, gerrymander, futurama,* and, to select a fairly recent New York example, *litterbug,* are additional illustrations of this process.

All these modes of growth summed together would hardly suffice to give us the enormous number of words that appears in modern civilized vocabularies. Foreign borrowing, normal coinage, root-combination, would lead to a fairly normal process of orderly growth. They would give us, in the case of English, an increase of perhaps a hundred thousand words within a century. There is another force at work that has expanded our vocabulary and those of other languages from the modest two or three hundred thousand words of a century ago to the million of today. It is this force that bears watching.

As human activities grow and develop, each tends to create its own specialized set of words, familiar only to the people engaged in that particular field. These special class or occupational languages are most responsible for the overflowing tendencies of today's national tongues. Medicine, law, government, education, science, engineering, technology, business, theology, military affairs, all have created their own specific languages, practically incomprehensible to anyone outside the profession or calling. A complete dictionary of the language must register such words. It is these words that constitute perhaps as much as seventy-five per cent of the vocabulary of every civilized language, that overwhelming majority of words of the language which you and I do not know and will never know, unless we engage in the field of activity in which each segment of those words is used. It is these words that are growing at an abnormal rate of speed, cluttering up the language, breaking it up into a series of class languages or jargons, making it mutually incomprehensible to people who should be linguistically united. Some of the jargon terms are vaguely familiar to those engaged in other occupations, others are as completely foreign as a foreign language.

Do you know precisely what your doctor means when he tells you you are suffering from "bilateral perorbital hematoma," or from "torticollis"? The chances are you do not. In one case it is a black eye, in the other a stiff neck, but these are not the official medical terms for the conditions described. The language of the law speaks of "escheat" and "escrow," and of writs of "mandamus" and "certiorari." If you are widely read you have come across these terms, but unless you are a lawyer you probably do not know precisely what they mean. Your automobile repairman speaks glibly of "bushings" and "gaskets," "clutch plates" and "piston rings"; you have a vague, uncomfortable feeling that the objects these words denote all form part of your car, which you drive with moderate skill; but unless you have gone into automotive mechanics your knowledge is likely to be inadequate. Educators love to speak of "integration," "correlation," and "motivation," terms which are legitimate enough, and even generally comprehensible; but they use them in a sense that escapes you, unless you are steeped in the lore of pedagogy. Linguists, who are among the worst sinners in the matter of terminology, have devised such mouthfilling terms as "morphophonemic," "sandhi," and "compound juncture," which mean less than nothing to the layman. Each field of sports has its own terminology, mysterious to the uninitiate. Labor of the organized variety has "lackey" and "check off," "featherbedding" and "graveyard shift." The steel industry has "blooms" and "skelp," coal-mining has "breeze," seedgrowers speak of "rogues," musicians use "god-box" and "licorice stick" and "frisking whiskers." Psychoanalysis has long spoken of "egos" and "ids" and "libidos," but then along comes dianetics to tell us of "basic-basics" and "engrams," "prereleases" and "audits," "somatics" and "time-tracks." You will note that the same word may be used in two or more unrelated fields of human activity, in widely different meanings. "Basic" is used in linguistics (Basic English), "audit" in business, "somatic" in medicine. It is all very bewildering. When you think you have acquired a new word, it turns out that you have gained control over a single one of its acceptances, and that it still eludes you in many others.

Reference is sometimes made in literature to the mysterious tongue of the Gypsies, a sort of double-talk that leaves the innocent bystander completely in the dark. Rodeo people have devised a vocabulary that no one but themselves can understand, a "waddy lingo" made up of terms like "appalucy" and "bulldogging," "to california" and "crowbait," "broomtail," "gunsel," and "quirley." The oil fields have such picturesque terms as "catskinners" (men who drive tractors), "cherrypickers" (small cranes), "mudhogs" (welldrilling pumps), "Christmas trees" (well heads), "roughnecks" (driller's helpers). A particularly fruitful jargon can be found in the talk of railroad men. A caboose is known among them by any of these or a dozen other terms: "doghouse," "zoo," "brain cage," "perambulator," "glory wagon," "monkey wagon." An engineer is variously known as "Casey Jones," "highball artist," "eagle-eye."

The difference between jargon and slang is perhaps overprecisely defined as follows: jargon is that which remains within a certain occupational or social class and is generally unintelligible to outsiders; slang is what spills over into the general language of the entire population, so that it is normally understood. A minute's reflection will show the artificiality of this distinction. "Pigeon" for girl, "bratting" for baby-sitting, are part of the jargon of teen-agers; it is questionable whether the terms will be understood by the average adult. "To play ball with," "to be caught flatfooted," "hit and run" are baseball jargon terms that have passed over into general slang; the same can hardly be said of Dizzy Dean's use of "slud" as the past participle of "slide." From the argot of the underworld we have "C" for $100 and "grand" for $1,000, "ice" for diamonds, "boomstick" or "equalizer" for gun; some of these terms have been popularized by the movies to the point where they may be considered slang; others are not so certain.

§ § §

Slang itself is one of the greatest sources of vocabulary accretion, and perhaps the most powerful agent in language change. Slang wells up from the vivid imagination of the anonymous masses at all times and in all places, and supplies hosts of new words, some of which wither away and die within a few years of their creation (witness "23-skiddoo"), while others survive, thrive, and ultimately become part of the everyday colloquial tongue.

Slang displays all the characteristics of language, of which it is a legitimate part, whatever the purists may say or think. Some slang terms are borrowed from foreign sources, like "crank" and "cranky" (from German *krank,* ill), or "fresh" in the sense of impudent (from German *frech*). Others display a change in meaning ("bean" in the sense of "head"). Others are created by imitation ("his'n," "our'n," "your'n," formed in imitation of "mine" and "thine," which have a final -*n* sound). Many are downright creations, like "oomph."

Slang is a very ancient phenomenon. Sanskrit and Latin literary records, among others, show the use of terms that originally meant "dish" or "pot" in the sense of "head" (exactly like our term "crackpot"). Ancient Roman plays, particularly those of Plautus, made extensive use of the slang of the Suburra, the racy tongue of slaves and gladiators and the lower classes. François Villon, in the fifteenth century, made such heavy use of the *argot* and *jobelyn* of the Parisian underworld of his times that many of the terms in his poems are incomprehensible to modern French scholars. It is generally recognized that the Romance tongues arose not directly from the classical Latin of literature, but rather from the spicy Vulgar Latin of the masses, which only occasionally crops up in the less elegant Latin writers.

Slang, cant, jargon, colloquialisms, vulgarisms, all contribute new words to the existing languages, and do so at a swift pace. Other, older words drop out to make room for the newcomers, but not with the same speed. The net result is an over-all increase in vocabulary, which joins the other mighty streams arising from the coinage of words legitimately needed by the progress of science and invention, from the importation of foreign words that describe objects not previously known, and from the creations of literary writers. So the river of language, which a century ago resembled the Hudson above Albany, grows and swells by reason of these numerous tributaries until it becomes a veritable sea, in which we all run the risk of drowning.

This experience is common to all civilized tongues, without exception. Chinese is the vehicle of an ancient and honorable culture, yet Chinese, coming in contact with the habits of the West, has found it necessary to heap coinage upon coinage in order to keep pace with our modes of expression. At the proceedings of the United Nations, the Chinese linguists have been forced to create compound words, like "origin-matter-shot" for atomic bomb, "U-metal" for uranium, "man-sheep-butcher-kill" for genocide.

The following account given by Alfredo Schiaffini, who undertook to prepare a dictionary of new Italian words, is instructive since his experience is the same as that of lexicographers of all languages:

> When I opened the sluice-gates of my mind to the flood of words that clamored for admittance to my work, I was appalled. Where I had thought in terms of hundreds, I found myself faced with thousands and tens of thousands. Here were the capricious, petulant words of fashion and elegance, fluttering in swarms like butterflies; beyond, a mighty host of words of learned and scientific origin, marching with measured, haughty tread, like regiments of soldiers, neatly marshalled according to their fields of activity; then an insolent crowd of foreign words, driving before them, like captured slaves, native words whose places they had usurped; then a flock of new creations and coinages; and with them, the esthetic words of the new rhetoric, the specialized words of medicine, technology, engineering, economics, journalism, sport, all minor languages within a language. And last of all, an endless line of words proud of their native origin, which had grown up on our own soil, words from the vernacular and the dialects, which said to me: "If you take in these aliens, why not us? We may be rough and plebian, but we are rough as the diamond is rough before it is polished. Our roots are in the heart of the people!" Faced with these infinite hordes of words, I was on the point of quickly shutting the sluice-gates again

and forgetting about the whole matter; but then my sense of duty prevailed, and I girded myself for the task of sifting out the newcomers, one by one, decimating them as they entered.

Actually, the dictionary of new words that resulted from all this storm and stress runs to about 1,000 pages and over 20,000 words. The author, however, warns us that only one in ten got in.

§   §   §

Such, then, is the general picture of our word-civilization, which, as has been remarked before, duplicates our population problem and our range of activities. Is there anything we can do about the situation? Can we invoke the principles of a linguistic Malthusianism to restrain our word-population, so that the vocabulary of a given language may still remain within the reach of a reasonably cultured and intelligent individual? Or must we resign ourselves to seeing all the tongues of civilization break up into mutually incomprehensible class languages, professional and occupational jargons, sectional slangs; in short, separate languages?

What has already been done in the way of exerting human control over language is little enough. The compilers of the older versions of Webster's Dictionary had devised an ingenious scheme for taking care of neologisms and slang words concerning whose ultimate survival there was some doubt. Such words, as fast as they appeared, were placed in the New Words section of the Dictionary, and left there on probation. If, within a stated time limit, they proved their ability to remain in popular use, they were granted permanent admission. In this fashion we had, in the earlier decades of the century, the admission to the language of *blimp, comeback, getaway, wangle, strip tease, zoot suit, soap opera, jitterbug, juke box.* Among the latest to be removed from probation were *cheesecake, corny, whodunit, gimmick, snafu, stooge, gremlin.* About ninety per cent of the New Words became permanent, for speakers seemed very loath to give up what they once had acquired. Since word-deaths are barely one tenth of word-births, the vocabulary thus continued to expand unceasingly. But most recent issues of the Dictionary now admit words without any formality or trial period.

Puristic devices, though frequently invoked, are of little help in limiting vocabulary. The fact that older editions of Webster's rated words as "colloquial," "vulgarism," "slang," was no deterrent to their use, even when it was practiced. "Good usage" is something that went out of style long ago if, indeed, it ever existed (many words that were substandard in Shakespeare's day were used by him in his plays, and thereafter became part of the standard language).

There would be one way of reducing our stock of words, but advocating it seems somewhat similar to advocating population reduction by the expedient of killing off every second inhabitant of the globe. If we were to cut down our range of activities, do away with some of our branches of learning, occupations, customs, and habits, the vocabulary peculiar to those activities would soon shrivel away and disappear. Something of the sort occurred after the fall of the Roman Empire, when many forms of activity that had been carried on in the classical world became obsolete and were not immediately replaced. Substitute activities, however, were eventually found, and gave rise to new vocabularies. Nobody would advocate the obliteration or even the curtailment of our modern civilization by the hydrogen bomb merely in order to have the satisfaction of seeing the language restored within reasonable bounds.

The solution of the world's linguistic troubles would therefore seem to lie in a series of empirical remedies, none complete in itself. Word birth control is emphatically not the solution. It could not be enforced, and would in any event tend to lead us back to the days of obscurantism and purism. No nation wants either bootlegged words or restrictions upon its linguistic freedom.

We must in part learn to live with our expanded vocabulary, just as we have learned to live with our expanded population. A hundred years ago, an agglomeration of humanity such as is found in our super-cities today would have been unthinkable. People felt crowded if they did not have at least a few acres all to themselves. Today the living accommodations of many of us are cramped, but we enjoy benefits that compensate us for the crowding. It is the same with language. We must like our wealth of words, or we would not create so many of them. Therefore, why not learn to live with them? The expansion of the individual's vocabulary is something that is accessible to each and every one of us. Why must we be satisfied with a 30,000, or 60,000, or even a 100,000-word vocabulary? We have at our disposal an educational machinery that was not available in the days of our forefathers. We can learn the words we need to learn.

A process of intelligent discrimination is, of course, necessary. There is no need for the layman to know by memory all of the complicated terminology of medicine or the law, which the physician or the lawyer has on the tip of his tongue. All that is required is that we have access to those words and their meanings, through the proper works of reference, so that if we come across them and need to know them we may be able to find them easily. The vocabulary of everyday life has expanded and will expand, and we can expand our knowledge with it. Specialized vocabularies can be left to the specialists and to the works of reference. This is just ordinary, practical common sense.

Since the specialists in the various fields are responsible for the technical vocabularies of their own fields, it might be urged upon them to try to simplify rather than complicate those vocabularies, not only for the purpose of making them at least partly accessible to the layman, but also for their own sake. Specialists are unwilling to admit it, but they are often bewildered by their own or their colleagues' linguistic creations. In every field of specialization, at least half the terminology is superfluous and redundant. There is a multiplicity of expressions for the same thing, and a tendency to coin great mouth-filling phrases that have no real purpose save to dazzle the layman. Would it be too much to ask that this tendency be repressed?

When we come to spontaneous creation, which reveals itself in popular slang, or in the picturesque jargons of certain manual occupations, there is little that can be done. Such vocabulary comes from the very wellsprings of human nature, and is as inherent and irrepressible as is the human longing for freedom and self-expression.

Finally, we must not forget that there is always the possibility, though not the likelihood, of a reversal in trend. Such a reversal is not at all to be wished for. It would be attended, as it always has been, by a disappearance of material things and activities. The sort of atomic warfare that is sometimes envisaged by many of our scientists and military experts would lead to an impoverishment of our vocabulary, just as it would lead to an impoverishment in all other fields. With the collapse of cities and buildings, industries and businesses, amusements and pleasures, the vocabularies of those disappearing ways of life would tend to vanish, too. As mankind went underground and resigned itself to a new form of cave-dwelling existence, a cave-dwelling jargon would arise to take the place of all the variegated sets of words we have at our disposal today. Civilization would sink, and our word-stock would sink with it. Bleak poverty would strike at everything and everyone, the language included.

Let us therefore rather accept the present state of affairs and count our blessings, linguistic as well as material, intellectual, and spiritual. The embarrassment of wealth is preferable to the embarrassment of poverty.

Changing Times—
Changing Words

Two forces working in opposite directions tend to reshape the American language at the present time. One pushes the language into a standardized, conventionalized mold; the old regional accents and expressions are squeezed out of existence in favor of a universal, uniform American speech that becomes more and more the common medium of expression and exchange in city streets and country lanes alike. The other adds the spice of variety and never-ending novelty to the American vocabulary, breaking it up into separate tools for separate segments of the population. The strange thing about these two contrary forces is that they stem from the same areas of activity—promotional advertising and modern technology.

A second contradictory effect of the two currents issuing from the same sources is that while in a sense they vulgarize the language, they also tend to lift it into higher and more specialized spheres.

The language of promotional advertising must be nationwide in order to achieve its avowed purpose, nationwide sales. It is this language that pervades the chief advertising media—radio, television, the press, and particularly the magazines with national circulation. And it is this highly standardized language that exerts its powerful leveling influence upon both our spoken and our written tongue.

What are the characteristics of the language of advertising and promotion? First, it must avoid localism, both in accent and in form. It will not do, on a coast-to-coast hookup, to feature, save occasionally and for purposes of humor, the drawl of the South, the nasal twang of the Midwest, or the coarser features of the New York speech. Nor may the advertiser use, or permit to be used in his name, expressions that have valid meaning in one area and not in others, like the Southern *poke* for *bag*, or the Boston *tonic* for *soft drink*. The penalty is misunderstanding, ridicule for the product, and, worst of all, loss of sales.

What is the reflection of this advertising speech, standardized both in vocabulary and pronunciation, upon the speech of the listeners, viewers, and readers? Since we all unconsciously tend to imitate what we hear and read, the general effect is a leveling one. Linguistic fieldworkers report that there is a gradual disappearance of local features in the United States language, with a tendency toward uniformity of both vocabulary and sounds.

The promotional language, however, also tends toward the least common denominator in educational and cultural standards. This, too, is a necessity. If you speak or write over the heads of your audiences, you may antagonize and lose vast segments of potential buyers. Therefore, the niceties of pronunciation and grammar are avoided. The advertiser or newscaster does not hesitate to violate the taboos of formal grammar. Torrents of ink have flowed over "like a cigarette should," but there are plenty of other violations. Split infinitives and dangling participles abound. How often do you hear "It is I" or "Whom did you see?" on radio or television? How often does a radio or TV speaker pronounce the first *r* in *February*, the first recommended pronunciation in Webster's? Have you ever, on radio or television, heard *margarine* pronounced with the *g* of *good*, as both orthography and etymology would seem to require?

Vulgarisms and colloquialisms are seldom created by the language of advertising, but they are undoubtedly sanctioned, perpetuated, and given wide currency by that language. This is also true of the written language of the advertising press. An advertiser is warned by numerous readers that the product he is trying to sell is a *chaise longue*, not a *chaise lounge*. His reply? "The way I have it in the ad is the way ninety per cent of my customers both spell and pronounce it; the customer is always right!"

§   §   §

Up to this point, we could go along with the promotional language on two separate counts: (1) it is not the function of advertising to act as a watchdog over the language; (2) English, particularly American English, has no set standard save that of general usage.

But there is another sin of which the advertising language is guilty, one that results in deliberately created distortions and confusions. Spellings like *nite, kool,* and *E.Z.* are bound to throw immature minds into uncertainty. It may be only a newspaper story, but the fact that a whole roomful of school children wrote *duz* for *does,* and defended it on the ground that that was the only way they had seen the word spelled on TV seems to point to a definite danger. The following charge was made by Dr. Francis Shoemaker, professor of English at Teachers College of Columbia University: "Through the forceful presence of very effective advertising, our spelling is being markedly altered. For the purpose of a pun or a quick advertising phrase, the sound of the words we use is gradually being changed. This powerful force in society is in many respects operating contrary to the aims of education."

Perhaps he had in mind a distortion of spoken *Hello* which made it sound more or less like *halo.* I can testify that this bit of radio advertising threw at least one foreigner into confusion. "Am I pronouncing *hello* correctly," the foreigner inquired, "or should I pronounce it as I hear it on the radio?"

There is the matter of misspelling and mispronunciation of foreign names and words, *Boiardi* presented as *boy-ar-*DEE, *Buitoni* as *beaut-*OH-*nee, La France* with *la* pronounced as in French and *France* as in English, *zizanie* offered with stress on the initial syllable. But it is an advertiser's privilege to mispronounce his own name if he chooses to do so, and foreign loan words may be anglicized as to sound and stress. There is little sanction, however, for comparatives and superlatives formed on nouns, as evidenced by *coffee-er coffee,* *macaroniest,* and even *egg-noodliest* (first in the field of this family, to the best of my knowledge, was *peanuttiest;* but here the coiners at least had the grace to turn the noun into an adjective before offering us its superlative form). Rank coinages of the type of *beef-a-roni, rice-a-roni, noodle-roni,* violate every canon of composition, derivation, and word formation. But of what avail to condemn the name if the product sells?

§ § §

In the previous chapter we discussed the rapid expansion of vocabulary caused by the multiplication of modern man's activities, the thousands and hundreds of thousands of words which crowd into our comprehensive dictionaries from all our specialized fields, and which no one but the specialist really knows how to use. The vocabularies of science and technology are often appropriated and given new twists by the advertisers. When you are faced with droves of words like *hydromatic, irradiated, irium, arnel, duratex, oldsmobility, beaverette,* and *naugahyde,* you can either disregard them, or accept them on faith, like magic words, or look them up and try to find out what they actually mean. In the last eventuality, they serve a truly useful purpose, since they add to your own personal word-stock and general understanding of the world around you. But in far too many cases they turn out to be nothing but euphonious sales pitches, sizzles meant to sell the steak.

The impact of the language of science and technology, even when it registers upon the individual, is largely superficial, to the extent that it affects only the vocabulary. not the sounds or grammatical structure of the language. The tongue of promotional advertising, on the other hand. has a subtler, deeper, and more pervasive influence. It reaches far more people. It tends to unite the speakers and obliterate their geographical and even their social divisions, which is perhaps a blessing. It also tends to vulgarize (debase is perhaps too strong a term) their spoken and written language. But this, in the case of a language like English, is not an irremediable catastrophe.

It definitely tends to stress the short, pithy, monosyllabic elements of vocabulary (save in the case of the prestige, mouth-filling, pseudoscientific terms described above). A prime example of the love for the monosyllabic was the quick shift heard on the radio from "If headaches persist or recur frequently" to "If headaches hang on too long or keep coming back." In like manner the "halitosis" of a decade ago has given way to "bad breath." But this again is no real drawback.

It tends to do away with the personal pronouns *it* and *they,* favoring instead the endless and often annoying repetitions of the name of the sponsor or product, to the point where in the year 2000 a foreign chronicler of American English may write: "Personal pronouns, which are still quite alive in British English, are obsolescent in American. This is particularly true of the third person neuter pronoun *it,* which only the older generation of American English speakers occasionally uses today. Instead, Americans prefer to repeat the noun over and over again, often with ludicrous effects."

On the other hand, the deliberate creations of the advertising language, while often brief, breezy, monosyllabic, phonetically spelled, and grammatically incorrect, are almost as often of the lengthy, magic-word variety, designed not so much to enlighten as to ensnare.

§   §   §

In a free society, there is not too much that can be done about all this, even if one wanted to try. Yet the speakers, hearers, and viewers, who too often seem to be the supine recipients of advertising outrages, have their own sweet, if unobtrusive, ways of wreaking vengeance on their tormentors.

Only recently "Mother, I'd rather do it myself!" became such a hilarious byword that it was quickly withdrawn from circulation. Something similar seems to be happening to "We must be doing something right!" The legal representative of a firm that has as its trade-mark *sanforized* complained because a writer had innocently assumed the existence of a complete verb *to sanforize*. The offending infinitive was withdrawn from print, but there is no way of withdrawing it from word-of-mouth circulation. A representative of the Gillette safety razor company inquired whether there would be any way of inducing the language academies of various foreign lands to pronounce that *gillette* should not be used as a synonym for *safety razor* of any brand. The answer was that even if the academies were to make such a pronouncement, the speakers would pay them no attention whatsoever.

In matters of language, the consensus of the speakers is the court of last resort. Even mighty advertising, with all the resources at its command, must bow to that court's decisions.

Shall We Bring English Up To Date?

"Who Do You Want for Mayor?" was the title of a two-column editorial in a New York daily newspaper; the editorial centered not upon the Mayor, however, but upon the "who." The question had previously appeared in another column of the same paper, and irate correspondents had pointed out that "whom," not "who," was the proper form to use. The editorial refuted this view. In the abstract, the editor agreed with his critics. In practice, he upheld his columnist on the ground that "whom" was high-hat, and that the popular tongue had long since outstripped the rules of grammar.

"Shall" and "will," "ain't" and "it's me" were among the forms cited as additional examples of the language of the people at loggerheads with the language of the scholars. According to grammar, "shall" and "should" ought to be used after "I," or "we"; "will" and "would" after "you," "he," "she," "they." How many people reply "I shall" to the question "Will you do it?", or say correctly "We should have seen him if he had been there"? Fortunately, the spoken language permits such abbreviations as "I'll and "we'd," which do service for most controversial forms.

In an Army manual designed to teach English to French speakers, a critic found the sentence: "I laid on the bed for an hour." Triumphantly he brought it to the notice of the proper authorities, only to be told that the error was deliberate. "That's the way ninety per cent of the G.I.'s say it," was the answer. "Yes, we know it's ungrammatical. But we want *spoken* English, not book English."

One modern manual of language instruction says: "Language is the way people speak, not the way someone thinks they ought to speak." Another writer of the same school preaches: "If you say 'I seen him' or 'It ain't me' in certain circles, you won't be invited to tea again; but if you say 'I saw him' or 'It isn't I' in certain other circles, you will draw just as much social disapproval and ridicule."

§   §   §

Should the English language be revised and brought up to date? Should we, as the editor of the daily newspaper advocated, grant official recognition to "ain't," "It's me," and "I seen him"?

In some countries there are national academies whose primary function is to take care of the language, and prescribe which words and forms are or are not permissible. The French Academy (founded in 1635 under the sponsorship of Cardinal Richelieu) shortly before the war brought out a grammar of what was, in the opinion of the members, good current French usage. Straightway one of the greatest historians of the French language (Ferdinand Brunot) wrote a complete volume in which the Academy's norms of grammar were torn to shreds on the rocks not only of popular, but even of literary usage. The controversy still goes on.

The Italian *Accademia della Crusca* has been in existence since 1582. Its name means Academy of the Chaff, and the theory is that it should separate the wheat from the chaff for what concerns language and slang. No self-respecting modern Italian writer pays it the slightest attention.

The English-speaking world has no Academy. The Oxford Dictionary in Britain, Webster's in America, are the chosen authorities as to what is good language, what is slang, and what is a colloquialism. "Ain't" was described in the older Webster's as "colloquial or illiterate." Schoolmarms have been endeavoring to eradicate the "ain't" habit since time immemorial, all to no avail.

If the mountain won't come to Mohammed, Mohammed might go to the mountain. Grammatical usage might be revised and redefined so as to admit "ain't," "will" in the first person, "I laid on the bed," "it's me," "between you and I," and a few dozen other such "incorrect" but extremely widespread forms. But the very fact that we have no unified central authority, no language academy, stands in the way.

It's all very well for popular dailies to advocate certain forms that are current in the United States. But are they also current in Britain and other English-speaking countries? Even if they are ("ain't" is a case in point) will our British cousins, notoriously more conservative than we are, agree to legitimize officially what has been sanctioned by usage? If not, we run the risk of giving a punch in the jaw to the English-Speaking Union and setting up a separate American language.

Some may say that the latter already exists. "Her Majesty's Government are in favour of this measure" causes us to grin. Yet our own Constitution uses a plural complement with a collective noun: "The Senate shall choose their other officers." But our spoken language has shifted from the plural to the singular, while the British have lagged behind.

There is no unity in the English-speaking world over pronunciation, spelling, or the meaning of words. Above all, nowhere in the entire English-speaking world is there an authority to impose uniform rules of grammar, pronunciation, spelling, and vocabulary that must be accepted by all speakers who wish to escape the charge of being what the linguists euphemistically term substandard.

§   §   §

The editorial in question hints that spelling reform would be a good thing. *Tonite, foto,* would pass muster with the editor; but not *thru.* Why not?

Spelling is indeed the most anachronistic and confusing feature of English. A good deal of it goes back to the days of Chaucer, when *knight* was not pronounced NITE, as it is today, but KNIKHT, very similar in pronunciation and spelling to German *Knecht,* to which it is related. Shakespeare spelled his name in three different ways, and Andrew Jackson is said to have remarked that it was a poor mind that could not think of more than one way to spell a word.

For every single point of grammar that needs bringing up to date, there are thousands of cases of spelling. Spelling is the nightmare of the foreigner trying to learn English, since he never knows from the written form of the word which way the pronunciation is going to jump. It is a terrific burden upon our own people, who have to learn to spell through grammar school, high school, college, and university, and then, after achieving a Ph.D., still have to look up the spelling of a word in Webster's.

George Bernard Shaw, Britain's great advocate of spelling reform, is believed to have originated the joke to the effect that *fish* can be spelled *ghoti* by using the *gh* of "enough," the *o* of "women," and the *ti* of "nation." The late Senator Robert L. Owen of Oklahoma, our own crusader in this field, used to say that all we had to do to make English the universal language would be to adopt a rational, phonetic system of spelling, like his Global Alphabet. There is little doubt in my mind, however, that he was underestimating the difficulties.

In spelling, as in everything else, we lack a central authority, a language academy. In language, as in law, English speakers go by precedent, not by code. They blunder along if they are Americans, and muddle through if they are British. When the Archangel Gabriel blows his final horn, it is likely that half our English speakers will justify themselves with "It isn't I who did it," while the other half will phrase it, "It ain't me who done it." Both, probably, will be adjudged not guilty.

A Standard for English

In those countries where the spoken language is fairly well represented by its written counterpart, relatively little time has to be devoted to the problem of spelling. The alphabet is presented, then the students are instructed simply to use it logically, to put their words together, and when they hear a certain sound to use a certain letter. This becomes impossible in languages like English and French, where the same sound may be denoted by as many as fifteen or sixteen different combinations. In countries where this discrepancy exists, we are compelled to go through a very long, troublesome, time-wasting process of learning how to spell and how to read and write. This means in turn that all the time that is devoted to learning how to read and write has to be taken away from other more factual subjects. It has been suggested by many observers that one of the reasons why English-speaking children run somewhat behind those of other countries in their acquisition of factual subjects is that they have to devote so much time to the study of their writing system and to the correlation between speech and writing.

Under the circumstances, is spelling reform desirable? Is it possible? How can we go about it? For many years a group called the Simplified Spelling Association, with branches in both Britain and America, has been advocating some sort of phonetization and modernization of English spelling. So far, their efforts have not borne noticeable fruit, largely because people are traditionally minded and don't care to be disturbed in the habits they have acquired.

But there is, to my mind, a much deeper underlying reason for the lack of interest in spelling reform, and that is that English is not only a language of conflicting spellings and pronunciations, but also a language of conflicting pronunciations quite aside from the spellings. It is not a standardized language. There are dialects in English, and none of these dialects is official. There is no acceptance, in America, of the British Queen's English, and there cannot be acceptance in Britain of an American standard that doesn't even exist. If you glance through Webster's dictionary (it doesn't have to be the new, permissive Third Edition; the old, uncontested Second Edition will do quite nicely) you will find plenty of varying pronunciations. Where the two are given as being equally good, it doesn't matter whether you use an Eastern pronunciation and make no distinction between *horse* and *hoarse,* or go Midwestern and distinguish between the two. It doesn't matter whether you make a threefold distinction as is done in the East between *marry, merry,* and *Mary,* or pronounce the three exactly alike, as is done in the Midwest. We do not have a standard.

Now, if we undertook to give English a phonetic spelling, the question would arise, phonetic of what? This would be a representation of what form of pronunciation? Which would be the standard? The first move in any spelling reform would be to establish some sort of English standard in the matter of pronunciation, and this would mean that we would have to classify certain sounds and certain forms of pronunciation as "correct" and "incorrect," something that American linguists are very unwilling to do. Yet, without this, we are going to have, in any revised spelling, the same sort of difficulty we have today: spelling that does not reflect pronunciation.

§   §   §

A good many of the spelling reformers are compromise-minded, willing to accept a partial reform and to settle for less than complete phonetization. For example, some of them would accept *nite* to represent *night*. Actually, that is not at all a phonetic spelling. By any sort of scientifically phonetic standard, *nite* would be pronounced NEE-tay. That type of reform is no reform at all. It would only cause greater confusion, nationally and internationally.

The next problem in spelling reform is to determine how far it should go. Do we want to hang on to our present Roman alphabet of twenty-six characters? If so, we are not going to have enough characters to go around, because there are at least forty separate distinctive sounds, or phonemes, in the English language (the number may run up in the case of certain spoken dialects). What shall we do about the sounds for which we don't have symbols? With our present alphabetic notation, the only thing we can do is to use combinations of symbols, or digraphs. But the minute we do that, we are getting away from the sound-for-symbol correspondence that is viewed as the phonetic ideal. Ideally, the sound of *th* in *think,* being a single sound, should be represented by a single character. When we use two letters to represent it, we are using a digraph in writing to indicate what is a monophone in speech. Ideally, a monophone should be represented by a monograph, or single symbol.

If we use a scientific type of alphabet such as the International Phonetic Alphabet (commonly abbreviated to IPA), we will have precise correspondence of symbol for sound. But that will mean that the people, particularly the adult generation, will have to learn to read and write all over again. When the average English speaker is confronted with something in English written in IPA characters, his reaction is normally one of horror. The victim of the experiment says: "Why, this isn't English! I can't read it!" He would have to unlearn what he already knows, and then learn all over again. Naturally, this process would not be necessary for young children who were starting from scratch. They would learn to read and write by a natural, easy, simple process that would take very little time and labor. But the adult, who has already put a vast investment of time and labor into learning the present irrational system of spelling, balks at the relatively small amount of time and labor that would be involved in his learning a new and more rational system. Since adults, not young children, rule the world and determine policies at any given historical period, we are stymied by this objection.

So far as the mechanics of the reform are concerned, our political structure, which has so many advantages over others, offers a major stumbling block. In most of the world's countries, the central government is in charge of education. If the central government wants to put through an innovation, it can do so by fiat. This has happened, within this century, in Turkey and in the U.S.S.R. It happens, on a minor scale but in recurrent form, in the case of languages like Portuguese and Norwegian. It is in the process of happening in mainland China as well as on Formosa. But in countries like America and Britain, education is a function of local government. This means that English reform would have to be put through state by state in America, school district by school district in Britain. Again, lack of standardization blocks our way.

A great deal has been and is being said about English as an international language. Gallup and similar polls indicate that English is the leading contender for that post in countries where it is not the national, popular tongue. But there is a note of warning that appears in a Japanese poll of 1960. Well over sixty per cent of the Japanese students at the University of Tokyo and of all foreign tourists in Japan who were polled indicated English as their choice, but the majority of them specified "modified English." What did they mean by modified English? Had they meant Basic English, with a reduced vocabulary, the chances are they would have said so. The "modification" they had in mind could bear on only two things: grammatical structure or spelling. The grammatical structure of English does not present insurmountable complexities. The chances are that these adult, educated critics were referring to the complexity of our spelling.

§   §   §

Would it be worth while for native English speakers to phonetize their language so that it might be accepted for international use? Before we reply enthusiastically in the affirmative, let us recall that phonetization is not as simple a matter as it seems at first glance. Regardless of what system is adopted, we have to standardize before we phonetize, at least for international use. We could not let English run amuck internationally the way it does on its various native soils. When you go out calling you keep your child under some sort of reasonable control; the same thing would have to apply to English if we ever allowed it to spill outside of our own borders and become an international tongue, under penalty of seeing English turn into a new version of Latin after the fall of the Roman Empire, giving rise to a host of separate, mutually incomprehensible new languages that would duplicate, on a far vaster scale, the Romance languages of today.

We would therefore have to standardize English even before we attempted to phonetize it. We would have to pick out all sorts of compromise pronunciations. We would have to take each word, give it a standard pronunciation form, and then proclaim: "Now *this* is correct. Anything else you want to use you may, but with the full knowledge and realization that you are using an incorrect and substandard form."

Is the inducement of World English good enough to entice English speakers into submitting to the two major operations of standardization and phonetization?

CHAPTER NINE

A B C D E F G H I J K L M N O P Q R S T U V W X Y Z

The Problem of Spelling Reform[1]

The reform of English spelling is a question that has long agitated speakers and writers on both sides of the Atlantic. Without going into the lengthy and thorny history of the problem, the pros and cons, the hundreds of solutions that have been proposed, particularly within the last fifty years, we may point to the real progress achieved by Noah Webster in his *American Dictionary* of 1828 (to him we are indebted for our *labor, theater, traveled, check, draft, defense, plow,* as against the British *labour, theatre, travelled, cheque, draught, defence, plough*), and to the noble but unavailing crusade of George Bernard Shaw, who even left prizes for suitable solutions, which no one has won to date.

Groups and associations interested in spelling reform exist both here and in Britain. In addition, several weighty intellects have been devoting time and labor to the question. Among them are the Rev. Frank Laubach, who has constructed dozens of writing systems for the use of backward groups, and George Hecht, publisher of *Parents' Magazine,* whose interest in the topic is based primarily upon a desire to ease the task of schoolchildren who have to learn to read, write, and spell.

[1] This chapter presents one facet of the spelling reform situation that is seldom mentioned and generally minimized, but has a good deal to do with opposition to spelling reform.

There is almost universal consensus that a rational, phonetic system of spelling would cut years from the learning time of English-speaking children and make it possible for them to concentrate on factual subjects, as do the children of other countries more fortunate in this respect, since they use languages where the divergence between the spoken and the written form is slight, and the process of learning to read, write, and spell takes a year or less.

Britain has taken the official lead in spelling reform experimentation in the schools by devising a so-called Augmented Roman Alphabet which, despite some glaring imperfections, seems materially to cut school time devoted to the reading-writing process. Augmented Roman is a sort of semi-phonetic alphabet consisting of a larger number of characters than the twenty-six ordinary Roman. The children who are taught reading and writing by this device fall rather easily into the practice, since its symbols have an approximation to the sounds of speech. After learning to use Augmented Roman, they are later shifted over to standard spelling; but by this time they have acquired the twin habits of reading and writing, and the adjustment is claimed to be far easier than if both the reading and writing process and the inconsistencies of traditional English spelling were presented at the same time.

Many objections to total spelling reform have been advanced on both sides of the ocean. Chief among them is the problem of what to do with our existing body of printed material, which would have to be scrapped and reprinted, at the cost of infinite money, time, and labor, and which under any circumstances would have to be retained until the reprinting process were completed, so that for a period of time that could well run into decades schoolchildren, students, and foreign learners would have to familiarize themselves with both systems, the old and the new.

There is another, largely unspoken objection which psychologically looms even larger. Most of the systems so far advanced—and this includes both the semi-phonetic Augmented Roman of Britain and the thoroughly phonetic, sound-for-symbol system of the IPA—find it necessary to adopt or devise many new and unfamiliar symbols. The reason for this is that English, as spoken by either Britishers or Americans, contains at least forty significant sounds or phonemes, while the alphabet we use has only twenty-six characters. Our present system of spelling gets around this hurdle by using an inordinate number of digraphs. On a straight symbol-for-sound correspondence, such as the IPA, both *this* and *thing* would appear in three letters of unvarying value, instead of four or five letters that may have different values in other words. But this can be done only at the cost of introducing new characters (ð for the *th* of *this*, θ for the *th* of *thing*, ŋ for the *ng* of *thing;* actually, this is how the two words look in IPA transcription: ðis, θiŋ).

This in turn means: (a) that the general public would be faced not merely with new spellings, but with strange characters, whose value would have to be painfully acquired; (b) that provision would have to be made in all printing machines, present and future, for the new additional characters, with the corresponding obligation upon linotype operators to familiarize themselves with a new and more complex keyboard; (c) that our present typewriters, with their familiar keyboard arrangement of letters and symbols, would have to be either scrapped and replaced or radically rebuilt, and all people who now operate a typewriter by the touch system would have to undergo new training.

This is perhaps the crux of the matter. Those who have had occasion to view the reluctance, bordering on terror, with which the adult or semi-adult American student approaches a strange alphabet, such as the Russian, Greek, or Hebrew, will realize at once what sort of a problem this shift poses. New generations, starting from scratch, would find the new system extremely easy and thoroughly logical; but many of our less gifted adults would find it impossible to cope with.

The reluctance of American typesetters to use any but the standard letters of the alphabet is proverbial. Books containing strange characters often have to be sent abroad, as the process of setting them here is too costly and time-consuming. Serious American newspapers, such as *The New York Times,* make it a practice to print foreign words and names without their appropriate suprascript and subscript characters, umlauts and cedillas, tils and accent marks. Mergenthaler and other printing lists have all the strange and unusual characters and all the non-Roman alphabets; the trouble is in getting your printer to order them in time and then to set them. As a rule, the author gets them only in his final page proof, and then usually with plenty of errors.

Professional and non-professional typists, who are thoroughly accustomed to the standard keyboard, would find it almost impossible to retrain themselves to use a keyboard with strange and more numerous characters. If anyone doubts this, let him try to use a typewriter with the letters rearranged on the basis of their frequency of occurrence in another language.

This, to my mind, is the primary, or at least the initial obstacle in the way of any sort of phonetic spelling reform. It must be considered also that the new and unfamiliar characters would call for handwritten script forms, with appropriate ligatures. These so far have not been devised, and if they were, would lead to new complications, since not everyone would form them the same way. Think of what difficulties are encountered in deciphering some forms of handwriting even now, then project these into what would happen if we tried to standardize the sixteen or more new and unfamiliar characters that the IPA alphabet offers for as many phonemes of English.

What would really satisfy everybody would be a system that would thoroughly and precisely represent the forty primary sounds of the language, yet use only the twenty-six standard letters of the present English Roman alphabet, augmented, at the most, by one or two additional characters already appearing on all typewriter keyboards and printing fonts. This can be accomplished provided we are willing to use a number of digraphs. But the combinations must be such that they will under no circumstances be misleading, and tempt the reader to pronounce the two letters separately (consider, for instance, what happens to the *th* combination in *other* and in *hothouse,* or to *ph* in *phone* and in *uphill*). There is a simple way of achieving this objective. It calls for utilizing all twenty-six letters, plus (but not necessarily) one additional keyboard symbol.

§　　§　　§

For the consonant phonemes of English, over half of our consonant letters could continue to be used exactly as they are used now: *p, b, t, d, f, v, r, l, m, n, w.* The sound now appearing variously as *k* (*key*), *c* (*cat*), *ch* (*choir*), *q* (*quire*) would invariably be represented by *k. G* would continue to have its present value in *get,* but never the sound it has in *general;* that sound would be represented by *j,* which would also serve in its present function (*jet*). *S* would cover all cases where it now appears unvoiced (*sit, fits*); it would also replace *c* before *e* and *i* (*cent*). Where present written *s* represents a voiced sound (*rose, girls*) it would be replaced by *z,* which would also have its usual present function (*zero*). *C,* no longer used in words like *cat, choir, cent,* would invariably stand for the *ch*-sound of *church.* The *sh*-sound of *shore, sure, nation,* could be represented by *x,* which is used in that function in several languages, Portuguese among them. The voiced palatal sound of *s* in *pleasure,* which is now sometimes transcribed as *zh* (though that spelling never occurs in English), could be represented by *q.* If this seems unusual and strange, let us recall that the *pleasure* sound is of very rare occurrence in English, while the written or printed occurrence of the letter *q* is so rare that it is placed in the most inaccessible position on the keyboard. Most spelling reform systems, as well as those of constructed languages like Esperanto, simply scrap *x* and *q;* but why not utilize them, since we have them in our standard alphabet?

Y would have its present value in *yet, boy,* where it is a glide sound that combines with the preceding or following vowel to form a diphthong. It would not be used in cases where it represents a pure vowel sound, as in *very, many, rhythm;* there it would be replaced by the vowel symbol *i.* Three consonant digraphs would appear, with two of which we are already thoroughly familiar: *ng,* used as it is now used in *sing; th,* to represent the unvoiced sound of *thing; dh,* to represent the voiced sound of *this.*

At this point, before going on to the changes that would have to be made in the vowels, we might pause to see how the language would begin to look in its new spelling. *Bid, pit, din, tin, vet, went, fit, sit, hit, get, kid, thing, jet, led, met, nest, yes, yet, rip, men, sing, wed* would all appear unchanged. But *gist* would be *jist, chrism* would be *krizm, this* would be *dhis, chip* would be *cip, bids* would be *bidz, boys* would be *boyz, cent* would be *sent* (yes, exactly the same as our present *sent;* but we have plenty of homographs-homophones right now, and the context tells which is meant: "He was very pale," "He was beyond the pale").

Here are three new spellings that really call for an effort, and at the same time present in advance some of the vowel changes: *pleasure* would be *pleq'r; sugar* would be *xug'r; nation* would be *neyx'n; general* would be *jen'r'l* (or instead, we might have *pleqeur, xugeur, neyxeun, jeneureul*).

§   §   §

For the vowels, it must be noted that some sounds popularly assumed to be vowels are not pure vowels but diphthongs, or combinations of two vowel sounds. This is true of *o* in *note, a* in *late, i* in *fight, u* in *union.* Our antiquated spelling represents them with a single letter symbol because they were once pronounced as pure vowels.

True pure vowel *sounds* in English are generally put at between twelve and fourteen. The experts are not in full agreement, and there are discrepancies of pronunciation among the American dialects, as well as between British and American English. We therefore strike a compromise, based on cultivated American Eastern pronunciation, which need not be binding upon all English speakers, and may be subject to revision if the new spelling were ever to be standardized for universal use.

Our true vowel sounds are either long or short. In our present system, short vowel sounds are generally indicated by a single vowel letter (*it, met, not, son, sun, hat*). The short vowel sound of *look* is usually indicated by the digraph *oo,* which also does service for its long counterpart (as in *tool*). The indefinite vowel sound of *the* in *the man* (as uttered in rapid, unstressed speech), the unstressed initial vowel sound of *arouse,* the two unstressed vowel sounds of *general,* though they are all the identical neutral sound (called *shva* by the linguists), are indicated by whatever vowel letter happens to be etymological (*general,* for instance, is spelled the way it is only because it comes from Latin *generalis;* so far as pronunciation is concerned, it could just as well be spelled *genural, genirel, genorel,* or half a dozen other ways).

There is no reason to change the representation of short *i* and short *e,* so words like *it* and *met* would remain unchanged. When we come to the *o* of *not,* most American speakers use what is phonetically *a,* while most British speakers use open *o,* which IPA represents by an inverted *c*. For American use, *a* would be a better representation, all the more since we have another use for the letter *o;* therefore, *not* would become *nat, pot* would become *pat,* etc. The letter *o* should be reserved for the *o* of *son* and the *u* of *sun.* Phonetically, this sound is not quite *o,* and IPA represents it by an inverted *v*. But it comes closer to *o* than to any other vowel sound for which there is a standard alphabetic symbol; also, most foreign speakers who do not have the sound in their sound scheme tend to replace it with open *o.* Therefore, *son* and *sun* will both appear as *son, but* will appear as *bot, cut* as *kot*. On the other hand, *u* can be used for the short vowel sound of *look, took* (*luk, tuk*). This leaves us with no more vowel symbols, and two more short vowel sounds. The first is that of *hat, land*. Here we have a ready-made digraph offered to us by our ancestral Anglo-Saxon, *ae* (*haet, laend*). Last of all, we come to the neutral vowel sound of unstressed *the, a* in *arouse,* the last two vowels of *general,* etc. This is the weakest sound in the language, but also one of the most frequent. In certain positions, many dictionaries represent it by an apostrophe (Webster's, for instance, has *ab'l* for *able*). If we follow their lead, *the* becomes *dh',* *arouse* becomes *'rawz, general* becomes *jen'r'l*. But if we wish to retain the apostrophe to indicate elision and possessive forms, we may borrow from French the digraph *eu,* which in French represents a vowel sound close to, but not identical with ours. We could therefore have *dheu, eurawz, jeneureul*.

Each short vowel sound of English has a more or less exact long counterpart. These long vowel sounds are indicated in our present system by an anarchical mixture of spellings. The long sound that pairs off with the short *i* of *it* may now be spelled *i* (*machine*), *ee* (*feet*), *ea* (*each*), *ei* (*receive*), *ie* (*believe*), etc. The long sound that pairs off with the short *e* of *met* may be spelled *e* (*there*), *a* (*bare*), *ea* (*bear*), *ai* (*fair*), *ei* (*their*), etc. The long counterpart of the short sound heard in American *not* is regularly represented by *a* (*far, father*). There is a long *o* sound that pairs off, though not precisely, with the short sound of *son, sun,* and it may now be spelled as *o* (*horn*), *aw* (*awful*), *a* (*all*), etc. The same *oo* that is used for the short sound of *took* is at present used for the long sound of *tool*. The vowel sound of *hat* may be lengthened if a voiced consonant follows (*had* vs. *hat*), but the lengthening does not always take place, and in any event the distinction between the two does not lend itself to misunderstanding. Lastly, the short neutral vowel of unstressed *the* has as its long counterpart (again not too precisely) the *i* of *girl,* the *u* of *curl,* the *ea* of *pearl,* etc.

At the present time it happens quite frequently, though not consistently, that we represent a long vowel sound, particularly in exclamations, with an added *h* (*ah, eh, oh, ooh*). Why not utilize in consistent fashion this *h* added on to a short vowel to indicate its lengthened counterpart? If we do this, we shall represent *machine, feet, each, receive, believe* by *m'xihn* (or *meuxihn*), *fiht, ihc, risihv, bilihv. There* (or *their*), *bare* (or *bear*), *fair* (or *fare*) will be represented by *dhehr, behr, fehr,* respectively. For *far* and *father,* we shall have *fahr, fahdh'r* (or *fahdheur*). *Horn, awful, all* will be represented by *hohrn, ohf'l* (or *ohfeul*), *ohl. Tool* will be *tuhl.* We may, if we wish, represent the somewhat lengthened vowel sound of *bad,* as against the shorter one of *bat,* by *aeh* (*baehd*); but this is not necessary, since the lengthening is a matter of individual choice and never lends itself to confusion between two words. Lastly, *girl, curl, pearl* will be indicated, according to our choice, by *g'hrl, k'hrl, p'hrl* or by *geuhrl, keuhrl, peuhrl.*

§ § §

This disposes of our simple phonemes, or primary sounds. But spoken English also has many diphthongs. Diphthong sounds consist of two vowel sounds pronounced in immediate succession, so that one glides into or off the other. The most common diphthong sounds of American English are the ones heard in *low* or *open;* in *lay, bait,* or *late;* in *high* or *dry;* in *boy* or *oil;* in *how* or *house.* Actually, there are as many diphthong possibilities as there are possibilities of putting a *y-* or *w-glide* before or after a plain vowel sound, long or short.

The following examples will show the proposed representation of most English diphthongs. For the current *yon, yes, Yiddish, young, union,* where a *y*-glide precedes a short vowel sound, we shall have *yan, yes, Yidix, yong, yuny'n* (or *yunyeun*). For *yard, year, yore* or *your, you* or *yew, yearn,* where the *y*-glide precedes a long vowel sound, the representation will be *yahrd, yihr, yohr, yuh, y'hrn* (or *yeuhrn*). For *want, went, wit, wonder, won* or *one, wolf,* where a *w-glide* precedes a short vowel, we shall have *want, went, wit, wond'r* (or *wondeur*), *won, wulf.* For *where, ware, we, weary, ward, woo, word,* where the *w*-glide precedes a long vowel, the representation is *hwehr, wehr, wih, wihri, wohrd, wuh, w'hrd* (or *weuhrd*). For *I, my, aisle,* where the *y*-glide follows a short vowel sound, we shall have *Ay, may, ayl.* For *eight, say, late,* the forms will be *eyt, sey, leyt.* For *oil, boy,* we shall have *oyl, boy. How, house* will be *haw, haws. Note, toad, low* will appear as *nowt, towd, low.*

In a few instances, English offers triphthongs (vowels preceded by an on-glide and followed by an off-glide): *wait* or *weight, wight, white, wow, woe.* These will be represented by *weyt, wayt, hwayt, waw, wow,* respectively.

Our frequently used written combination *wh,* which reverses the order of the spoken sounds, would be replaced by a phonetic *hw,* so that *when* would appear as *hwen.*

The role played by the letter *h* in the proposed set-up might be described in linguistic jargon as characterized by complementary distribution. Initially, *h* would retain its present aspirated value (*how, house* appearing as *haw, haws*). Used after a vowel, it would indicate that the vowel is long (*ih* for what now appears as *ee, ea, i, ie, ei,* etc.; *oh* for what now appears as *o, a, aw*). In the very few cases where *h* has its aspirated value inside a word, a hyphen would be used to separate the *h* from the preceding vowel: *hat-haws* for *hothouse; op-hil* for *uphill; '-hoy* (or *eu-hoy*) for *ahoy.* There would never be any possibility of confusing the two functions of *h,* as they would occur in positions which would invariably be different.

§   §   §

As a sample of how the new system would function, here is the opening paragraph of this chapter. Note that the transcription is completely done by ordinary typewriter, without the use of a single outside symbol or diacritic mark.

Yet it portrays the sounds with fidelity and symbol-for-sound (or digraph-for-sound) correspondence:

Dh' (Dheu) rifohrm av Inglix speling iz ' (eu) kwesx'n (kwesxeun) dhaet haez lohng aejiteyt'd (aejiteyteud) spihk'rz (spihkeurz) aend rayt'rz (rayteurz) an bowth saydz av dhi 'tlaentik (Eutlaentik). Widhawt gowing 'gen (eugen) intu dh' (dheu) lengthi aend thohrni hist'ri (histeuri) av dh' (dheu) prabl'm (prableum), dh' (dheu) prowz aend kanz, dh' (dheu) hondredz av soluhx'nz (soluhxeunz) dhaet haev bin propowzd, partikyul'rli (partikyuleurli) widhin dh' (dheu) laest fifti yihrz, wih mey poynt tu dh' (dheu) rihl pragres 'cihvd (eucihvd) bay Now' (Noweu) Webst'r (Websteur) in hiz *'merik'n (Eumerikeun) Dikxon'ri (Dikxoneuri)* av eytihn twenti-eyt (tu him wih ahr indet'd (indeteud) fohr awr *leyb'r (leybeur), thi't'r (thieuteur), traev'ld (traeveuld), cek, draeft, difens, plaw,* aez 'genst (eugenst) dh' (theu) Britix . . .), aend tu dh' (dheu) nowb'l (nowbeul) bot on'veyling (oneuveyling) kruseyd av Johrj B 'hrn'rd Xoh, huh ihv'n (ihveun) left prayz'z (prayzeuz) fohr suht'b'l (suhteubeul) soluhx'nz (soluhxeunz), hwic now won haez won tu deyt.

PART THREE

a b c d e f g h i j k l m n o p q r s t u v w x y z

USAGE AND

THE DICTIONARY

TWO POINTS OF VIEW ON LANGUAGE, GRAM-
mar, and usage, one traditional and prescriptive, the other
permissive and descriptive, began to clash in the late 1920's. The
conflict was at first subdued, then grew louder, as both British
and American grammarians and lexicographers became involved.
It finally crashed out in the explosive response to the appearance
of the Merriam-Webster's Third New International Dictionary
of 1960. This was the signal for the outbreak of an angry controversy that raged for months in book review pages and even
editorial sections of newspapers and magazines.

On the surface, the discussion hinged largely upon the function of a modern dictionary. Should it merely record usage (and
if so, what kind of usage)? Or should it assume the duties of
an arbiter linguae, much like a European language academy,
and pontificate as to what is "correct," or at least desirable in
language?

Heated and far-flung as it was, the controversy was only a
symptom of the far deeper conflict that had been building up
over a period of thirty years or more. How should language
itself be viewed? An an unconscious activity, or as a product and
manifestation of the conscious human mind? As a blind physical
force, operating with the inevitability of the laws of nature, or
as a largely psychological function, as unpredictable as man
himself? Should language be subject to artificial restraints, or left
to seek its own course, even a destructive one? Is language to be
harnessed, or is it to be given free rein in the mouth of each and
every one of its speakers? Is usage simply a matter of a numerical
majority, or is it subject to a hierarchy of education and good
taste? Is there a utilitarian, practical side to the dispute? Will
the speakers gain more by giving language its head and allow-
ing it to run wild, or by placing it under a measure of control?
If the latter, who is to exercise that control?

The excerpts from book reviews that form the opening of this section outline the genesis and prehistory of the great American linguistic controversy of 1960–1. In part, they indicate an attempt to mediate between two conflicting points of view where, as it turned out, no mediation was possible.

The two final chapters review the problem in all its aspects, and bring its hidden background into the open. In a sense, they still represent a desire to effect a reasonable compromise between two extreme positions.

CHAPTER TEN

A B C D E F G H I J K L M N O P Q R S T U V W X Y Z

Leave Your Language Alone

It is Professor Hall's contention [in *Leave Your Language Alone!*] that there is no such thing as good or bad, correct or incorrect, right or wrong language; that there is no such thing as "written language"; that a dictionary or grammar is not as good an authority for your speech as the way you yourself speak; that words have no meaning, save as it is conferred upon them by the community of speakers; that all languages and dialects are of equal merit; that languages do not "decay" or become "corrupted," but simply change.

Professor Hall does not believe in linguistic academies or in the sanctity of grammatical rules. He would accept such forms as "you done it," "he don't," "that's his'n," in much the same fashion in which people accept holding the fork with the right hand instead of the left. Linguistic correctness, he avers, is a traditional, anti-democratic relic, and the "four-letter words" are fully justified in the speech of a ditchdigger.

Whatever the merits of this stand may be, it is a little difficult to reconcile some of the author's statements; e.g.: "some of us are inclined to think that because a habit, a custom or a thing is old, it must necessarily be better than something new" and "writing is definitely subordinate in historical origin to speaking." I also view with some suspicion his claim that gesture languages are simply more remote derivatives of speech; most linguists and anthropologists hold the opposite view. On the other hand, I cannot but heartily concur in his denunciation of modern English spelling and the waste of time it involves.

In view of the author's widely publicized revolutionary linguistic philosophy, I should expect him to come to equally revolutionary conclusions in his later chapter on Learning Your Own Language. Instead, we are regaled merely with a different motivation in teaching children "correct" forms. Don't tell them some forms are "right" and others "wrong," says Professor Hall, in effect: "We can easily make it clear to a child of ten or twelve that his advancement, his getting along, his getting whatever he wants out of life (whether that be personal advancement in any field, or money, or prestige, or intellectual or artistic pleasures) is going to depend to a considerable extent on his use of socially favored instead of disfavored forms."

The ideal language teacher's attitude is described as follows: "There's nothing wrong with 'it's me,' and it's in constant use by people whose usage is unquestioned; you are, however, likely to run into difficulties with some people who think that 'it's me' is incorrect, and when you're talking with people who are quite puristically inclined, you'd better avoid 'it's me' and use 'it is I,' even if it does seem somewhat unnatural."

All this smacks a bit of Milquetoastian hypocrisy and opportunism, but it does not differ radically from what has avowedly or covertly been done, in linguistic and many other areas, since time immemorial.

The claims of dictionaries, grammar books, and "guides to good usage" are described as "a pure fake and an imposture." Actually, by the author's definition, they are fully justified if we merely substitute for "what is right and what is wrong" the phrase "what is good for you and what isn't." Also, it is hardly true that in present-day America the use of "socially incorrect" forms necessarily leads to social condemnation and personal disadvantage. We need only refer to Ade, Ruark, Dizzy Dean, the sports writers, the composers of popular songs, to show that "incorrectness" very often pays, and pays well.[1] The stuffy, schoolmarmish attitude toward language that the author describes is pretty definitely a thing of the past, not only among linguists, but among the population at large, and this leaves Professor Hall, in a sense, tilting with windmills. It was his avowed intention to use psychiatric shock treatment on his readers; but in the end he pulls his punches, and finally leaves us with the admonition to use "correct" forms, not because they are "correct," but for our own crassly material good. . . .

[1] Since 1950, when this review appeared, the number of those who have cashed in on linguistic substandardness has so multiplied that the situation described by the author is completely reversed. One need only refer to such literary masterpieces as *Catcher in the Rye, Our Lady of the Flowers,* and *Who's Afraid of Virginia Woolf?* to be convinced that the more vulgar you get the better off you are, at least so far as money and literary prestige are concerned.

CHAPTER ELEVEN

A B C D E F G H I J K L M N O P Q R S T U V W X Y Z

Chamber of Horrors

In this diverting book [*Chamber of Horrors*], 'Vigilans' has gathered the full evidence in the case of the English-speaking peoples *versus* the creators of a speech variously known as Officialese, Barnacular, Whitehallese, or, on this side of the ocean, Gobbledegook, Federal Prose, or Federalese, both in its hieratic and its demotic varieties. Economese, Journalese, and Medicalese appear as prosecution witnesses, having signed a waiver of immunity; the tongue we of America know as Academese or Pedagese is also cited, though not specifically by name. The prosecuting attorneys are Sir Ernest Gowers, Sir Alan Herbert, George Orwell, B. Ifor Evans, Norman Riley, and Eric Partridge, for Britain; Paul Porter, J. R. Masterson, W. B. Phillips, Arthur Krock, and Peter Edson, for America; J. Y. T. Greig for South Africa. The charges range from circumlocution, use of long words and phrases, and general padding to euphemism, wooliness, and technicalism in language.

Jargon, Eric Partridge informs us in his elegant nine-page Introduction, is related to *gargle*, and goes back to an Indo-European root meaning throat. The throat, claims Maury Maverick, coiner of *gobbledegook*, is not that of a human being, but that of a strutting turkey. Faced with an alphabetically arranged list of linguistic horrors one hundred fifteen pages long, I am tempted to agree. The state's exhibits include such creations as *recategorization, civilianiza-*

tion, conurbation, subminiaturization, cubicalize, disintecticize, impermeabilize, pelletize, dilutee, demonstratee, separatee, liberee.[1] There are horrid compounds like *non-disincentive, overavailability, underdelivery,* and *superseniority,* as well as seemingly innocent but virulently active microbes of the type of *beddage, dissaver, quantify,* and *utilitor.* Word groups like *affirmative facilitation, depth interview, viable agreement,* and *top secret* round out the list.

Vigilans seems to have a special genius for picking out the pompous phrases dear to the bureaucratic heart: "deserving of serious consideration" (or "under active consideration"), "bring to a satisfactory conclusion," "scheduled for discontinuance," "serve no useful purpose," and, of course, the ineffable "in short supply." He perhaps weakens his case by the inclusion of more harmless administrative clichés, like "with reference to," "whether or not," "it will be found that." "Cause to be informed" is firmly entrenched in the legal language, and the circumlocution has a precedent, if not a justification, in the Latin *certiorem facere.* Nor can I altogether go along with the compiler in his criticism of certain Latin expressions like *agenda, data, per capita,* not to mention the diplomatic *casus belli, de facto,* and *status quo. Apartheid* may be merely the Afrikaans word for racial segregation, but when we see it in the columns of *The New York Times* we recognize it at once, and without further explanation, as the South African version of that phenomenon.

My academic conscience rejoices at the treatment accorded certain words affected by our Teachers College colleagues: *educator* and *maladjusted, motivation* and *integration, panel discussion* and *underprivileged* (in connection with the last, Vigilans, after giving the dictionary definition, "not privileged to enjoy certain rights theoretically possessed by all members of a community," editorializes: "No nonsense about earning the rights, or qualifying for the privileges!").

One considerable item in *Chamber of Horrors* worries me: the very large number of words and expressions which,

[1] Should we, at this late date, add President Johnson's *honoree,* countenanced by Webster 3?

while still "horrors" to the British compiler, have come to form part of our common American vocabulary to the point where they are accepted by practically everyone. I refer not merely to *and/or*, which the Georgia State Legislature recently tried to legalize, or to the *activate* which an oil concern is currently trying to ram down our throats (*activated gasoline*). Here are such words as *ascertain, beverage, divulge, donate, ideology, impact, outstanding* (said to be "a darling of American bureaucracy"), *partially, repercussion, state* (in "state your intentions"). Other expressions are neologisms, but we all use them: *backlog* (part-time), *basis, blanket coverage, blueprint, bottleneck, combat fatigue, conservative estimate, deadline, featherbedding, geared to, global, hospitalize, itemize, malnutrition, personnel, productivity, quota, recondition, stockpile, sabotage, winterize* (the compiler does not even seem to know that in America this term is applied to automobiles; he reserves it for aircraft and flying fields). Then there are the governmental words which to us are absolutely commonplace: *appropriate* (money), *briefing, cutback, decontrol, priority, rollback, inflation spiral*. In America, we speak currently of a person's *background;* we do not mind using *assist* as a synonym for *help* or *aid;* we are fond of "the teaching *field*," "pay *increments*," "*interdenominational* activities," "stamp-*vending* machines."

There is perhaps in Vigilans a touch of insularity, as well as a trace of purism (which does not keep him from using, in his own text, words like *jargoneer* and *scarified*). The English language is a tool designed for universal use. It accepts words and terms from non-English sources. It does not (and need not) restrict itself to words of one syllable. Above all, it has an unlimited capacity for growth, proved through the centuries since its inception. It is probable that it never will accept, at least in its more popular reaches, such words as *executivization* and *reflectorize;* but there is room in it for *vend* as well as *sell, impact* as well as *shock, beverage* as well as *drink, clarify* as well as *explain,* even for *public enemy* at one end and *a priori* at the other.

CHAPTER TWELVE

A B C D E F G H I J K L M N O P Q R S T U V W X Y Z

Usage and Abusage

For purposes of brevity and economy, the 1942–7 *Usage and Abusage* [Eric Partridge] has been cut down from 384 pages to little more than half that number. The concise version is, however, revised and augmented with several new entries. As in the earlier work, W. Cabell Greet has lent his aid with regard to American usage. The combination of these two distinguished names from the two major areas of the English-speaking world gives the reader a solid guarantee, not merely of accurate and thorough scholarship, but also of reasonable interpretation and handling.

Compare, for instance, the disposition of a word like *amoral*. Fowler, with characteristic intransigeance, says: "*Amoral*, being literary, is inexcusable, and *non-moral* should be used instead." Partridge equates it to *non-moral*, and offers the more prudent generalization that *a-* or *an-* for *not* should be prefixed only to Greek stems—a statement which has at least the justification of etymology. Elsewhere, the point is made that *demi-* should be used for French, *hemi-* for Greek, *semi-* for Latin, and *half-* for Teutonic words. (Has the author ever beheld that half-musical, half-jocular monstrosity, the *hemidemisemiquaver?*)

Valuable points of information abound, and only the man who wishes to remain blind can go through this volume without profit. To cite a few instances, there is the fascinating story of *nom de plume,* arising in English from a mixture of *nom de guerre* and *pen-name,* and thence traveling into the language it purports to be; the distinctions, not always observed even by professional writers, between *deprecate* and *depreciate, complement* and *compliment, principal* and *principle, its* and *it's, tortuous* and *torturous, each other* and *one another;* much-needed warnings against vogue words like *fabulous,* incorrect spellings like *diptheria* and *dipthong,* the singular use of *insignia,* rank vulgarisms like *and etc.,* the unnecessary use of prepositions like *up* and *down* in *burn up* and *burn down,* redundancies like the double conjunction *that* so dear to the heart of American speakers and writers. Rules for the use of the hyphen might be profitably read by some of our publishers and copy editors. That vague geographical entity, the Middle East, is given a sensible definition.

It is the sad duty of a reviewer to find what fault he can, even with a nigh-perfect work. Hence the following observations are offered not in a spirit of carping criticism, but in one of courteous dissent.

Partridge is perhaps over-severe with certain words. He labels "academic" such widely used terms as *fantastic, glamour, pattern, reaction,* and *urge.* Others, like *deem, dwell, fealty, selfsame, testimony,* are labeled "archaisms." "Literarisms" include *converse, deft, fleece* (in the sense of *cheat*), *wilderness,* while among "elegancies" we find *divulge, garb, garments, individual, retire.* (In some cases, British usage subtly differs from American in these respects.) Even *Ethiopia* falls under his "archaic" classification, despite the fact that it is the official name of the country.

Elsewhere he is somewhat inflexibly British, though he never even remotely approaches Fowler in that respect. He prefers the spelling *Barbadoes* to *Barbados,* despite the origin of the name (*Higos Barbados,* bearded figs, which grew on the island). He condemns as "affectations" *Gand, Lyon,* and *Marseille* (*Ghent,* after all, is as Flemish as *Gand* is French, and just what does the incorrect English *-s* add to the other place-names?). *Quadra-* is said to be "always wrong"; yet *quadragesimal* and *quadratic* cannot be denied. He calls "distressing" the use of the preterite for the perfect in American speech, which is a widespread linguistic phenomenon paralleled, for instance, by Spanish among the Romance tongues. Under "Plurals, un-English," he enjoins us to use *-s* and *-es* for foreign words: *"stilettos,* not, as in Italian, *stiletti";* this could be carried to such lengths as to give us *spaghettos* and *raviolos.*

American usage is, on the whole, very accurately described, though I cannot quite agree with the statement that *"indorse* is used and recommended in the U.S.A. to the exclusion of *endorse."* Among typical colloquial and slang Americanisms whose omission I notice are *drunk* as a noun, *proposition* as a very vulgar verb, the spelling *vittles (victuals,* however, is described in full), the novel and priceless *irregardless,* which could have complemented *irrespective,* and the regional, spoken-language *any more* with an affirmative verb ("it gets so cold in the evenings any more").

As a short-cut guide to correct, yet sensible English usage on both sides of the Atlantic, there is hardly any substitute for this little volume, which displays, along with perspicacity of choice and precision of content, the author's customary sense of urbanity and humaneness.

CHAPTER THIRTEEN

A B C D E F G H I J K L M N O P Q R S T U V W X Y Z

But What of
American Usage?

A European scholar recently remarked to me that there is a striking parallel between a nation's view of law and the same nation's view of language. The Roman tradition, he claimed, passed on to the nations descended from Rome a legal code which may on occasion be too lax or too severe, but which is fixed and precise. The Anglo-Saxon lands have inherited instead a tradition of "common law," working largely by precedent. "You are not right or wrong, guilty or not guilty in the eyes of the law by reason of fixed standards," he said, "but only by virtue of a series of decisions, often in conflict, made in similar cases across the centuries by judges who themselves relied upon earlier decisions. In like manner, when it comes to language, the Frenchman, Spaniard, or Italian can rely upon a ruling of his language academy and safely pronounce a certain form, spelling, pronunciation, or grammatical construction to be right or wrong. All you people of English speech can do is to refer to a vague, uncertain something known as usage, something that bears to language about the same relation that precedent bears to law."

§   §   §

In language, it was not always thus. The older generation among us still recalls the prescriptive, normative grammars of our youth, by whose dictum something you said or wrote was "right" or "wrong," and this despite the complete absence of an English-language Academy throughout our whole history. As a matter of fact, both Margaret Nicholson's *Dictionary of American-English Usage* and Fowler's *Modern English Usage,* from which it stems, blissfully combine the term "usage" with the unequivocable adjectives "right" and "wrong." It is perhaps only in the most modern American works, of which the Evans's book [*A Dictionary of Contemporary American Usage*] is a fair sample, that "usage" triumphs, and "right" and "wrong" are all but eliminated. But even the Evanses occasionally speak of "acceptable" and "unacceptable" uses.

By its very nature, usage lends itself to a variety of interpretations. In vain do our modern American grammarians seek to circumscribe and limit it by defining it as "the language of the educated people" (who is and who is not educated, in these days when practically everyone knows how to read and write, and most young people have gone to high school?), or the "standard language," to which an undefined "substandard" is opposed. How are we to determine usage? By a nose-counting process? We have become self-conscious about using the words "right" and "correct," which the modern school of American grammarians abhors, but does this make *laid* "standard" in the use quoted earlier (" I laid on the bed")?

All this is not being said in a spirit of criticism, but merely to indicate what thorns strew the path of one who would compose a dictionary of modern Anglo-American or American usage. "Language changes!" says Dr. Evans. True. The trouble is that it changes unevenly. An innovation may be accepted by some of the speakers, not by others. Then the question comes up: What is the standard? Shall we tolerate every innovation, however irrational or freakish? Shall we accept it only when it has penetrated the upper crust? Shall we regard those who say "I laid on the bed" and "I ain't got none" as ignoramuses? Or, conversely, shall we condemn as hopeless old fogies those who say "Whom did you see?" and "It is I"? Usage is such an elastic yardstick!

Fowler and, by reflection, Miss Nicholson display a certain reverence for the traditional. The Evanses are far more uninhibited and, by the same token, far more readable. They have, however, their own pet aversions. Few of the numerous familiar clichés escape their condemnation. Yet, come to think of it, are not clichés part of standard usage? Why avoid them? The very fact that they are "hackneyed" shows that they are very much in use. The doctrine of usage should require that we respect them and employ them to the full.

A complete review of these two highly interesting works would call for another book equal in length to both of them. Here is a sampling of random words and expressions:

according as—not mentioned by the Evanses; discussed by Fowler and even more thoroughly by Miss Nicholson, who brings in a contrast with *according to*.

ago—omitted by the Evanses; discussed by Fowler and Miss Nicholson, but without reference to the fairly common use of *ago* in the sense of *before* or *previously* ("He told me last Friday that he had seen him five days ago.")

ample—Fowler and Miss Nicholson claim that it should be used only with abstract words (we should not say, for instance, "We have ample water for drinking"). The Evanses limit themselves to claiming that *ample* implies "more than enough."

any more—I have long been intrigued by this interesting tidbit, used in parts of the Midwest, even by very cultured speakers, in an affirmative sentence, with the meaning of *now* or *at present* (see page 101). The Evanses describe it as regional, while Miss Nicholson and, more understandably, Fowler, make no mention of it.

ascend up—The Evanses bring out the interesting point that this expression is redundant, even though it appears in the

King James Bible. This would seem to knock out one of our main props of authority.

at death's door—like many other expressions, this is described as a cliché, and the Evanses suggest that we avoid it. But why?

cavalry-calvary—The interchange in this couplet has long disturbed me. The Evanses, too, are troubled by it, but not our other authors.

carry—In the sense of to take a person somewhere ("He carried me to the dance") this, too, is a regionalism, appearing in the South. No mention of it is made.

climb up; climb down—These are justified by the Evanses on the ground of popular usage, with literary samples dating back to 1300. Miss Nicholson grudgingly admits *climb down,* despite the purists' claim that it is an absurdity. Fowler ignores both expressions.

continue on—We frequently hear this on radio. It represents, presumably, a blend of *keep on* and *continue.* No mention.

defense—Miss Nicholson alone points out the difference between the British and the American spelling (*defence, defense*).

February—Not a word anywhere about the horrible but widespread pronunciation *Feb'-u-a-ry,* sanctioned even by the older Webster as a second choice.

figure—Fowler pronounces any pronunciation but *fig'-er* pedantic. Miss Nicholson softens the blow to the extent of pointing out that *fig'-ure* is the normal American pronunciation. The Evanses do not concern themselves with pronunciation, but describe as questionable (is this a euphemism for incorrect?) such typical American usages as "to figure out," "to figure on," and "to figure that."

irregardless—The fact that this is condemned by both the Evanses and Miss Nicholson, but ignored by Fowler, would seem to indicate that this blend of *regardless* and *irrespective* has not yet spread beyond the Atlantic.

laboratory—Fowler prefers *lab'-ra-to-ry* to the common *la-bo'-ra-to-ry*. Miss Nicholson describes the first pronunciation as American, the second as British.

lousy—No mention is made, even for purposes of condemnation, of this very common slang term, or of its partner *swell*. Is this not ignoring the facts of language?

margarine—Disdained by the Evanses, this word finds Fowler and Miss Nicholson at loggerheads. The former says it was practically unknown to the educated classes before the war, and therefore left to shift for itself among the ignorant; "but now that we all know the substance, its *g* is coming into its own." The latter says that hard *g* is only occasionally used in Britain, and practically never in the United States.

marital-martial—This couplet goes with *cavalry-calvary,* though the confusion occurs more frequently in writing than in speech. None of our authors mentions it.

siege—The fact that this word very often appears in print as *seige* (influence of *beige,* perhaps?) is recognized, at least by implication, by Miss Nicholson, who labels it "so spelled." The same is done with *supersede,* which so often appears in print as *supercede.*

susceptible of—Only the Evanses make mention of this expression, which they equate with *susceptible to* (quick reaction to a stimulus). Webster makes a clear distinction between "susceptible of proof" and "susceptible to infection."

tortuous-torturous—This confusion, not mentioned by Fowler, has evidently not yet broken into the British press. That it has unfortunately infected America is shown by both the Evanses and Miss Nicholson.

Because perhaps of my Italian background, I object rather strenuously to Fowler's high-handed statement that "the old established *nn* is recommended" in *Sienna, Siena.* Miss Nicholson has at least the grace to admit that *Siena* and *Sienese* are preferred in the United States for the proper noun and adjective, though even she holds out for *sienna* as a color. Despite all sections in all three books dealing with Didacticisms and Foreign Plurals, I still think foreign spellings should be respected, particularly when they make no difference in our own pronunciation. In like manner, I find no justification for *salami* (*salame* is the correct Italian form; *salami* is the plural, and means several sticks of *salame*); and I loathe and despise such double pluralizations as *macaronis* (admitted by Fowler, Miss Nicholson, and Webster!). These liberties taken with foreign loan words smack of linguistic colonialism.

§   §   §

The above list will give some idea of what is included in our two most recent dictionaries of American usage, as well as what is excluded from them. These works are both interesting and useful. The Evans's book is, in addition, good non-fiction reading, by reason of the straightforward views expressed and the dry sense of humor that seems to emanate from the authors. The two dictionaries can hardly be described as complete or exhaustive, but for this the authors cannot be justly blamed. The English language is, to use a brand-new cliché that will undoubtedly incur the wrath of Dr. Evans, a many-splendored thing, with infinite gradations and ramifications. Even the longer *Oxford English Dictionary,* with its many volumes, is incapable of telling the entire story.

CHAPTER FOURTEEN

A B C D E F G H I J K L M N O P Q R S T U V W X Y Z

That Dictionary

Language, like time, marches on. But language far out-strips time in its progress. Noah Webster's first unabridged dictionary, published in 1828, had 70,000 entries. The 1961 Merriam-Webster has 450,000. Of these, 100,000 are new words and new word meanings since the Second Edition.

All languages are potentially equal, but the extent and range of a language's vocabulary reflect the state of civiliza-tion of its speakers, the activities in which they indulge, the material objects they create and use, the abstract concepts they evolve. Far from viewing with alarm our astounding language growth within the past one hundred thirty years, we should rejoice over this index of material and intellectual progress. At the most, we may wonder how many 2,720-page volumes will be required for the Merriam-Webster Un-abridged of the year 2000.

It is all very well to say that the average speaker knows and uses only a small fraction of the total number of words listed. The words are there, at his disposal; and a certain proportion, however small, of our vocabulary increase must perforce rub off on even the most illiterate speaker. Merriam-Webster's publicity catch-phrase, "the greatest vocabulary explosion in history," has plenty of justification. Examples of it range all the way from *breezeway* and *split level* to *fringe benefit* and *sit-in,* from *air-lift* and *no-show* to *de-*

celeration and *astronaut*, from *beatnik* and *den mother* to *wage dividend* and *zen*.

There are many commendable features in this latest of vocabulary offerings [*Webster's New Third International Dictionary, Unabridged*]. Whether they are such as to justify the claim of "revolutionary techniques designed to make words meaningful to everyone" is perhaps debatable. Certain technical terms require far more than a dictionary definition to make them meaningful. Take, as a single example, and from the field of linguistics itself, the word *phoneme*. It is defined as: "the smallest unit of speech that distinguishes one utterance from another in all of the variations that it displays in the speech of a single person or particular dialect as the result of modifying influences (as neighboring sounds and stress); < the *p* of English *pin* and the *f* of English *fin* are two different phonemes >." Does this make the term *phoneme* meaningful to everyone?

One interesting feature of some of the entries consists of quotes from contemporary notables. These are said to be based on a citation file containing ten million words in context. General MacArthur, for example, is said to have clarified the fuzziness between *shall* in the sense of futurity and the sense of determination ("I shall return"). This brings up the question of authority, pointed up by the statement that the Merriam-Webster has been "the principal authority in courts of law, schools, and the U.S. Government Printing Office." The compilers would undoubtedly say that the dictionary's authority is based on usage, but the question insistently comes up: Whose usage? That of John F. Kennedy, or that of Joe Doakes? *Ain't*, we are told, gets official recognition at last as "used orally in most parts of the U.S. by cultivated speakers." With tongue in cheek, perhaps? Of course, *ain't* has a long and honorable tradition and has consistently appeared in dictionaries, both British and American; the new Merriam-Webster boasts of the fact that the label "colloquial" has been dropped, thus sanctioning the "informality of modern English." This is all to the good, but it leaves me wondering how far the process of informality can go before it incurs the charge of outright vulgarism.

It is obviously impossible to "review" the new Merriam-Webster in the same sense that one reviews an ordinary volume. But this question of usage, authority, colloquialisms, and vulgarisms set me off on a train of thought that led me to look up the series of obscenities and scatologies popularly covered by the expression "four-letter words," in comparison with an earlier edition at my disposal, that of 1884. Surprisingly, some of the words appearing in 1961 appear also in 1884 (with a "vulgar" label, of course). Even more surprisingly, a few words omitted from the 1884 edition are also omitted in 1961, despite their copious appearance in numerous works of contemporary literature as well as on rest-room walls. Why this residual prudishness? Ought not a dictionary based on usage to face the facts of life? The precise equivalents of these particular words appear in several foreign-language dictionaries in my possession, and even in a few bilingual dictionaries designed for college use!

As against deliberate omissions, there are accidental ones. Under the heading of *don* used as a noun I find both the British academic and the Spanish use (indicative of the fact that perfection is not of this world is the coupling of *don* with a preceding *signor* as "a Spanish courtesy title"). I do not find the Italian-American gangster slang acceptance ("He is a don of the Mafia"). Omitted also is Clare Booth Luce's colorful *globaloney*, which still enjoys deserved circulation today.

Inconsistencies in treatment appear. Why is *spaghetti* said to have plural -*s*, while *ravioli* and *rigatoni* are given -*i* plurals? From the standpoint of the language of origin, all these nouns are already plural. If usage is alleged as a defense, then I must regretfully report that the same people who say (and write!) *spaghettis* also say and write *raviolis*.

To illustrate the difference between the original 1828 and the modern 1961 editions, sample pages of the two are offered, containing definitions of the word *shake*. Despite the fact that the publicity speaks of "every strata of society," I must agree with the writer that the expansion in meaning of the word is little short of startling. Dozens of new meanings and uses appear, and they are exemplified by an impressive series of quotes ranging from Polly Adler to Virginia Woolf, and from *Police Detective* to *The New York Times*.

Yet I miss, in this new version, some of the features that appeared in the 1884 edition—sets of special tables at the end, and particularly etymologies for some personal and place names. Why does a work described as "literally all things to all users of the English language" give up even the mild attempts at such etymologies made by practically all earlier dictionaries, and even by the Merriam-Webster Collegiate? Are personal and place names not as much a part of the language as some of the common nouns that receive satisfactory attention? If anything, they stimulate curiosity even more. The difficulties attending their solution may on occasion be greater, but so is the satisfaction accruing to both researcher and reader.

Aside from missing etymologies, the general handling of place and personal names is surprising. The former are listed only in their adjectival function ("the Vietnam army"); the latter only if they have given rise to common nouns ("the johns" in the sense of "policemen").

Despite these and other criticisms that could and will be made, the 1961 Merriam-Webster will enjoy a healthy life, even if not too prolonged. It is the closest we can get, in America, to the voice of authority.

The Dictionary as a Battlefront

For some years, there have been more and more insistent rumblings from all sorts of quarters about the quality of the English imparted in our schools and colleges. Graduates of our educational institutions, the critics have charged, do not know how to spell, punctuate, or capitalize; to divide a thought concept into phrases, sentences, and paragraphs; or to express themselves, either in speech or writing, in the sort of English that is meaningful and acceptable. As a single sample of the many complaints that have been voiced, I may cite a friend who is a high official in WABC-TV: "Recently we interviewed over a hundred college graduates to fill a post calling for a knowledge of good English. Not one of them made the grade. None of them knew the rules of good writing, and none of them could express himself or herself in clear, simple, straightforward English sentences."

The blame for this state of affairs has consistently been put upon two branches of the educational world: the teachers of English and the progressive educationists. Books such as *Why Johnny Can't Read* are indictments of modern educational practice. A cultured lay writer, J. Donald Adams of *The New York Times Book Review,* said in his column of December 20, 1959:

If more parents who were themselves the recipients of a decent education could be made aware of the asinine statements about the teaching of the English language which are being spewed forth by today's educational theorists, there would be an armed uprising among the Parent-Teacher Associations all over the United States. It would be an uprising armed by common sense and hot indignation, and it would demand and get the scalps of those so-called educators whose indefensible doctrines are rapidly producing a generation of American illiterates. . . . The root responsibility for the decline in standards of English rests, I think, with the teachers of English in our primary and secondary schools, and even more so, with the teachers of education who produced them. . . . There is an organization called the National Council of Teachers of English, whose attitudes and activities constitute one of the chief threats to the cultivation of good English in our schools.

§   §   §

What critics of present-day methods of teaching English have in the past failed to realize is that the responsibility for the situation goes deeper than the departments of English and the teachers colleges. The practices of both are merely a reflection of the philosophy and theories of a school of linguistics that is in turn linked with a school of cultural anthropology of the equalitarian persuasion whose views color far more than the teaching of languages in general or English in particular.

As far back as 1948, in a *New York Herald Tribune* book review, Bernard De Voto came out with a blast at the cultural anthropologists for assuming that methods that seem to work with the Ubangi and the Trobriand Islanders would produce dependable results when applied to the English or Americans. But his was a voice crying in the wilderness. Few people were sufficiently specialized, or interested, to perceive the link between theories presented in scholarly books on anthropology or linguistics and practices that affect the daily lives of us all.

It was only with the appearance of the new third edition of *Webster's New International Dictionary, Unabridged* late in 1961 that the issues at stake became clear to the cultured, educated layman of America. For this there was a deep, underlying reason that reaches down to the grass roots of our mores.

Since the days of Dr. Johnson, who refused to embalm the language and thereby destroy liberty, English speakers have submitted to the Doctrine of Usage rather than to the Voice of Authority. But usage has its own canons. In Britain, something called the King's (or Queen's) English has been enshrined over and above local dialects that range from London's Cockney to super-cultivated Oxford, and from the harsh speech of the North Country to the mellifluous accents of Kent. In America there is no President's American, but there is the Dictionary. From the time of Noah Webster, Americans have been wont to dip into a dictionary, the more unabridged the better, to settle questions of usage and proper practice.

It may be stressed at this point that at no time did the compilers of the various editions of the Merriam-Webster, the most comprehensive dictionary of America, set themselves up as authorities or arrogate the right to tell the people what was correct and what was wrong in the matter of language. All they did was to record prevailing usage among the more educated classes. They listed and described plenty of variant regional pronunciations and words. They recorded, too, speech forms of the lower classes, carefully labeling them "colloquial," "substandard," "vulgar," or "slang." This was not meant to prescribe or proscribe the use of certain forms, but merely to inform the reader as to the distribution of their occurrence. The attitude of the earlier lexicographers seemed to be: "Go ahead and use this form if you want to; but if you do, don't complain if someone says you are using a slang term."

The new 1961 edition of the Merriam-Webster has many features to commend it. Not only does it list the multitude of new terms, technological and otherwise, that have entered the language in recent years; it also has the merit of listing, with full definitions and examples, word combinations that have acquired special connotations not inherent in their component parts. The older Webster's defines both "guilt" and "association"; but the new Webster's also gives you "guilt by association." This means that the new edition is a handier tool than the older.

But the new edition makes one startling innovation which has recommended itself to the attention of all reviewers and of the general public as well. It blurs to the point of obliteration the older distinction between standard, sub-standard, colloquial, vulgar, and slang. "Ain't," it says, is now used by many cultivated speakers; "who" in the accusative function and "me" after a copulative verb are of far more frequent occurrence then "whom" and "I," respectively; and, by implication, should be preferred. And this viewpoint goes right down the line. It led the editor of *The New York Times* to compose a passage that starts:

> A passel of double-domes at the G. & C. Merriam Company joint in Springfield, Mass., have been confabbing and yakking for twenty-seven years—which is not intended to infer that they have not been doing plenty work—and now they have finalized Webster's *Third New International Dictionary, Unabridged,* a new edition of that swell and esteemed word book.
>
> Those who regard the foregoing paragraph as acceptable English prose will find that the new Webster's is just the dictionary for them.

There is more: the older Webster's, insofar as it gave citations, used only established authors, recognized masters of the language. The new Webster's cites profusely from people who are in the public eye, but who can hardly be said to qualify as shining examples of fine speaking or writing. This leads another critic to complain that Churchill, Maritain, Oppenheimer, and Schweitzer are ranged as language sources side by side with Billy Rose, Ethel Merman,

James Cagney, and Ted Williams; Shakespeare and Milton rub shoulders with Polly Adler and Mickey Mantle.

Dr. Gove's defense, fully presented in a later issue of *The New York Times* that had thundered editorially against his product, is both able and forthright; a dictionary's function, he said in substance, is to record the language, not to judge or prescribe it. Language, like practically everything else, is in a state of constant flux. It is not responsible to expect it to remain static, to retain unchanged forms that were current at one period but are no longer current today. We have changed our point of view in many fields; why not in language? His defense is, in a sense, a counterattack against the forces of purism, conservatism, and reaction. Why disguise the true function of a dictionary by turning it into a tool of prescriptivism, a fortress of a language traditionalism that no one today really wants? Language, after all, is what people speak, not what someone, be it even Webster, thinks they ought to speak.

This both clarifies and restricts the issue. But an issue still remains. Should a dictionary be merely a record of what goes on in language (all language, both high and low), or should it also be not so much a prescriptive tool as a guide for the layman, to not merely what *is* usage, but what is the *best* usage?

A speaking community that has been accustomed for the better part of two centuries to rely upon the dictionary to settle questions of usage balks at finding all usage now set on an identical plane. The contention of the objectors is that there are different, clearly identifiable levels of usage, which it is the duty of the dictionary to define. Without necessarily using the terms correct and incorrect, they still would like to see a distinction made between what is better and what is worse.

§   §   §

In opposition to their stand, the new philosophy, linguistic and otherwise, seems to be summed up in this formula:

What is is good, simply because it is. Good and bad, right and wrong, correct and incorrect no longer exist. Any reference to any of these descriptive adjectives is a value judgment, and unworthy of the scientific attitude, which prescribes that we merely observe and catalogue the facts, carefully refraining from expressing either judgment or preference.

This relativistic philosophy, fully divorced from both ethics and esthetics, is said to be modern, sophisticated, and scientific. Perhaps it is. Some claim that its fruits are to be seen in present-day moral standards, national, international, and personal, as well as in modern so-called art, music, literature, and permissive education.

But we are concerned here only with its reflection on the language. The appearance of the new Webster's International has had several major effects. It has brought the question of permissiveness in language squarely to the attention of millions of educated laymen, who use the dictionary and refer to it for guidance. Without forcing a renunciation of Anglo-American reliance on usage rather than on the Voice of Authority, it has brought into focus the paramount question: Whose usage? That of the cultivated speakers, or that of the semi-literates? Finally, it has for the first time brought forth, into the view of the general public, those who are primarily responsible for the shift in attitude and point of view in matters of language—not the ordinary classroom teachers of English, not the educationists of the teachers colleges, but the followers of the American anthropological, descriptive, structuralistic school of linguistics, a school which for decades has been preaching that one form of language is as good as another; that there is no such thing as correct or incorrect so far as native speakers of the language are concerned; that at the age of five anyone who is not deaf or idiotic has gained a full mastery of his language; that we must not try to correct or improve language, but must leave it alone; that the only language activity worthy of the name is speech on the colloquial, slangy, even illiterate plane; that writing is a secondary, unimportant activity which cannot be dignified with the name of language; that systems of writing serve only to disguise the true nature of language; and that it would be well if we completely refrained from teaching spelling for a number of years.

If these pronouncements come as a novelty to some of my readers, it is the readers themselves who are at fault. The proponents of these language theories certainly have made no mystery about them; they have been openly, even vociferously advancing them for years, and this can be easily documented from their voluminous writings.

The real novelty of the situation lies in the fact that, through the publication of the new Webster's—compiled in accordance with these principles—the principles themselves and their original formulators, rather than their effects upon the younger generations, now come to the attention of the general public. Lay reviewers generally display their complete awareness.

Dwight Macdonald, reviewing the new Webster extensively in the March 10, 1962, issue of *The New Yorker,* after claiming that the "scientific" revolution in linguistics has meshed gears with a trend toward permissiveness, in the name of democracy, that is debasing our language by rendering it less precise and thus less effective as communication, goes on to say:

> Dr. Gove and the other makers of 3 are sympathetic to the school of language study that has become dominant since 1934. It is sometimes called Structural Linguistics and sometimes, rather magnificently, just Modern Linguistic Science. . . . Dr. Gove and his editors are part of the dominant movement in the professional study of language—one that has in the last few years established strong beachheads in the National Council of Teachers of English and the College English Association. . . . As a scientific discipline, Structural Linguistics can have no truck with values or standards. Its job is to deal only with The Facts.

Max S. Marshall, professor of microbiology at the University of California, writing in *Science,* March 2, 1962, says in part:

> Opposed to [believers in a standard quality of English], with several ringleaders at the head, is a group which goes back some thirty years, but has been actively proselytizing only in relatively recent years. These are the advocates of "observing precisely what happens when native speakers speak." These are the self-styled structural linguists, presenting language in a way so foreign that it might be imposed before users of the language discover its existence. . . . Gove declares himself flatly on the side of the structural linguists, calmly assuming, as do their ringleaders, that they are about to take over.

§   §   §

The principles of the American school of linguistics described above may come as a shock to some, but there is no need to be shocked. They are based upon definitely observable historical facts. Language invariably changes. Within our own personal experience we have noticed certain forms and expressions once considered slangy turning into regularly accepted parts of the standard language.

All that the American school of linguistics advocates is that we accept the process of change in language and submit gracefully to its inevitability. If we persist in hanging on to language forms and concepts that are antiquated and superseded, then we are merely subscribing to what they call "the superstitions of the past." We should be forward-looking, and progressive-minded. We renounce imperialism and colonialism in international relations, and admit nations like Ghana and the Congo to full equality with the established countries of Europe; by the same token, we should view the languages of the Arapahoes and the Zulus as being of equal importance with Latin and French. We believe in democracy and majority rule in political elections. Then, if a majority of the speakers of American English use "knowed," "I'll learn you," "between you and I," these forms are by definition standard usage, and the corresponding minority forms, though sanctioned by traditional grammars, are, if not incorrect, at least obsolescent.

It may be argued, as does our professor of microbiology in *Science,* that "weighing the speech of casual speakers with no pretense at expertness on the same IBM card as usages of topnotch writers of past and present is an example of what the modern linguist calls 'science.' Tabulation is not science. Public opinion polls do not settle questions of science, or even of right and wrong. . . . If the guttersnipes of language do more talking than professors of English they get proportionally more votes."

But the structuralistic linguists can easily reply that language is a matter of habit and convention, not of dogma or esthetics, and that if the basic purpose of semantic communication is achieved, it matters little what linguistic form is used. In engineering, calculations as to stresses and structures must be precise and correct, under penalty of seeing the bridge collapse. In medicine, correct dosage is essential, under penalty of seeing your patient die. But in language, the use of a substandard for a standard form seldom leads to irreparable consequences.

On the other hand, members of the American school of linguistics are not always consistent in the application of their democratic and equalitarian principles. In reply to his critics, Dr. Gove remarked that while comments in lay newspapers and magazines had generally been unfavorable, the learned journals had not yet reviewed the new edition. The implication seemed to be that favorable reviews from a few members of his own clique, read and approved by a small circle of professional structuralistic linguists, would more than offset the generally unfavorable reaction of newspapers like *The New York Times* and magazines like *The New Yorker,* which appeal to large audiences of cultivated laymen. This not only puts the process of democracy into reverse; it comes close to setting up a hierarchy of professional linguists acting as the Voice of Authority for a recalcitrant majority of educated people.[1]

§   §   §

There is no doubt in my mind that widespread localisms, slang, vulgarisms, colloquialisms, even obscenities and improprieties, should be duly noted in a comprehensive dictionary, whose first duty is to record what goes on in the field of language. Should such forms be labeled and described for what they are, not in a spirit of condemnation, but merely for the guidance of the reader? That, too, seems reasonable. If this procedure helps to slow up the inevitable process of language change by encouraging the speakers to use what the older dictionaries call standard forms, and discouraging them from using substandard forms, this impresses me as a distinct advantage. Too rapid and too widespread language change is a hindrance to communication. It lends itself to confusion and misunderstanding. The use of a more or less uniform standard by all members of the speaking community is desirable in the interests of efficiency rather than of esthetics. There is no question that within the next five hundred years the English language, along with all other languages spoken today, will be so changed as to be practically unrecognizable. This will happen whether we like it or not. But need we deliberately hasten and amplify the process? Between sudden revolution and stolid reaction there can be a middle ground of sound conservatism and orderly change.

Also, without being puristic to the point of ejecting "ain't" and kindred forms from a dictionary of recorded usage, it might be worth while to recognize the existence of a standard language, neither literary nor slangy, which has

[1] For further reading on this controversy, and abundant samples of articles and reviews that appeared in both general and specialized periodicals, see J. Sledd and W. R. Ebbitt: *Dictionaries and That Dictionary* (Chicago: Scott, Foresman & Co.; 1962), and J. C. Gray: *Words, Words and Words About Dictionaries* (San Francisco: Chandler Publishing Co.; 1963).

acceptance and is understood practically everywhere in the country, even if everybody does not use it in his own speech. Such phrases as "Them dogs is us'uns" and "I'll call you up without I can't," which an American structural linguist claims are good, meaningful language to him merely because they are uttered by some native American speakers, definitely do not form part of that standard language. By all means let us record them for our own information and amusement, but let us not try to palm them off on the public on the general ground that the native speaker can do no wrong, and that "correct" and "incorrect" are terms that can be legitimately applied only to the speech of foreigners attempting to use English.

Language is something more than a heritage of senti-mental value. It is an indispensable tool of communication and exchange of ideas. The more standardized and universal it is, the more effective it is. The more it is allowed to de-generate into local and class forms, the less effective it be-comes. It may be perfectly true that in the past language has been allowed to run its own sweet, unbridled course, with the chips falling where they might. We are now in an age where we no longer believe in letting diseases and epidemics run their natural course, but take active, artificial means to control them. In fact, we endeavor to control natural, physical, and sociological phenomena of all descriptions, from floods to business cycles, from weather to diet, from the monetary system to race relations. Is it unreasonable for us, far from leaving our language alone, as advocated by the American school of linguistics, to wish to channel it in the directions where it will prove of maximum efficiency for its avowed function, which is that of semantic transfer?

As for that other burning question, standards of writing, as apart from standards of speech, ought we not to recognize that until such a time as tapes, recordings, dictaphones, and films together replace our system of written communication, the latter should be viewed and treated with respect? Again, we need not let ourselves be led too far afield by purely literary or esthetic considerations. The written language, in a modern civilization, is practically on a par with speech as a communications tool. It is incongruous to see our American structuralistic linguists devote so much painstaking attention to phonetic phenomena like pitch, stress, intonation, and juncture, to the fine distinctions between "a light housekeeper" and "a lighthouse keeper," "an iceman" and "a nice man," and yet shrug their shoulders at correct spelling, punctuation, and capitalization. More misunderstandings have resulted from misplaced commas than from misplaced junctures, and a wrong spelling can be just as fatal as a wrong intonation.

Perhaps the time has come, in language as in other fields, for the return of reason, and its ascendancy over dogma, whether the latter be of the puristic or of the structuralistic variety.

Above all, there is need for sound, scientific consideration of *all* the facts of language, not merely that portion which happens to suit the tastes and inclinations of a small group. Language is more than a set of phonemes, morphemes, junctures, and stresses. It also happens to be our most important instrument of semantic transfer, and the common possession of all of us. If democracy means anything, we, the speakers, have the right to have our say as to how it shall be viewed and used, and not be forced to subscribe to the prescriptive excesses of what a European professor of linguistics has described as "the God's Truth School."

APPENDIX—WEBSTER'S THIRD IN THE CLASSROOM

For the teachers of English in our colleges, high schools, and even elementary schools, the appearance of the new dictionary brings up thorny pedagogical problems. A mathematics or science or history teacher can objectively prove that a correction made on a student's paper is justified. In the past, the English teacher could refer to Webster's for proof that a word, an expression, a form, or a spelling used by a student was, if not wrong, at least substandard. What can the teacher do now, short of leaving the pupil's language, both oral and written, alone and uncorrected? Let us imagine a conversation in the classroom:

PUPIL: "Teach, why did you mark this wrong?"

TEACHER: "It's substandard, Tom."

PUPIL: "But I looked up the word in Webster. It's given there, and it don't say nothin' about the word bein'—what you call it?"

TEACHER: "Just the same, it's substandard, which means it's not used by the cultured people of the community —just like the 'it don't say nothin' ' you used a second ago."

PUPIL: "But, Teach, didn't you learn us that the only guide to language is usage?"

TEACHER: "So?"

PUPIL: "So that's my usage! Ain't I got as much right to my own usage as anybody else?"

TEACHER: "But usage refers to the way of speaking of the more educated people in the community."

PUPIL: "You mean I ain't educated?"

TEACHER: "Well, I'll admit we're trying to educate you."

PUPIL: "Anyhow, I use that word all the time. So do all the other guys. Don't that make it usage?"

TEACHER: "Well, I don't want to establish class distinctions, but . . ."

PUPIL: "Aw, what's wrong with speaking like all the other guys do?"

TEACHER: "I suppose it's all right when you're speaking to your friends, but this is an English composition."

PUPIL: "You mean I should write different from the way I talk? But didn't you tell us the other day that what we write should be a refraction of what we hear spoken around us?"

TEACHER: "I said reflection, not refraction. Look, Tom, there's no point to prolonging this discussion. I'll mark you

right, since you have the backing of Webster's. All right?
No hard feelings?"

PUPIL: "It's O.K. by me, Teach! Gee, you're a swell
guy!"

§   §   §

One of the most prominent linguistic scientists envisages
the abolition of all instruction in spelling. Would it not be
at least equally logical to advocate the abolition of all instruction in English? With the triumph of the doctrine of
usage, amplified into "the native speaker can do no wrong,"
what does an English teacher have to teach his pupils that
the pupils don't already know? After all, "anyone who is
not deaf or idiotic has fully mastered his native language by
the end of his fifth year."

Teachers of English who listen to the siren song of the
structuralists should perhaps begin to show some concern
over the continuance of their own jobs, if not over anything else.

A Loss for Words

Two voices are raised throughout the land with the same frequency and insistence as that of the Turtle. One is the voice of the Advocates of Usage, the other that of the Custodians of the Language.

The Advocates of Usage, be their name Philip Gove, Bergen Evans, or any of a dozen others, tell us that language is what people speak, not what someone thinks they ought to speak. These people are willing to distinguish between what they call "standard" and "substandard" usage, but with the corollary that at any time, and under almost any set of circumstances, the substandard may turn into the standard. Without actually saying it in so many words, they hold that language should be subjected to a sort of democratic process similar to the one that prevails in our political life. If enough people say a certain thing a certain way, that is the way to say it (not, however, the "right" way, because "right" and "wrong" do not apply to language). Language is forever changing, and who are we to hold it back?

The Custodians of the Language range all the way from grammarians like the Fowlers to educators like Jacques Barzun and writers like Dwight Macdonald. They hold that there is a right and a wrong way of expressing yourself, and that the right way should be prescribed by works of a certain description, chief among them the dictionaries of the language.

The most recent clash between the two tendencies came at the time of the appearance of Merriam-Webster's *Third International Dictionary* of 1961, compiled by workers of the Advocates of Usage School under the direction of Philip Gove.

The main bone of contention has been fully outlined in the preceding chapter, which also hints at the implications of the controversy, which really involve an entire philosophy of life. Should there be a directing class, qualified as such by reason of intellect, education, and general culture, or should there be unbridled democracy, with a nose-counting process to determine what is good and bad?

It was argued that no matter how big a majority says that two and two make five, the undying truth is still that two and two make four. It was replied that language is not mathematics, a statement of principles that lie outside of and beyond man, but an instrument fashioned by mankind itself for mankind's own use, and subject to whatever changes its makers and users wish to make, even to the point of degradation rather than enhancement. On a totally different plane, it was demonstrated (the history of the language being fairly well known, at least in its more recent stages) that many of our language conventions in pronunciation, spelling, grammar, are of artificial and illogical origin, and that the anonymous users of the language have frequently gone to work and repaired the errors of their supposed betters. Such expressions as "like a cigarette should," "it's me," and "who did you see?" were traced back to writers of note.

§   §   §

It is hardly worth while to add fuel to the flames at this point, save for two perhaps secondary considerations. The first is that a dictionary of usage, if it aims to be that, should be utterly and relentlessly complete. It should not omit certain words on the ground that schoolchildren would look them up and gloat over them. The omitted words are in such widespread use that all people, including schoolchildren, have seen and heard them dozens of times.

But the omission of a handful of four-letter words constitutes only a minor part of the criticism. Far more important is the fact that other common forms of aberrant usage are similarly omitted, without apparent rhyme or reason. At what point does a vulgarism, or "error," or misspelling or misuse become too vulgar or erroneous for inclusion? Some of the omissions are very widespread. Failure to report such "wrong" forms would seem to imply strong condemnation on the part of the compilers, translated into unwillingness to give them greater currency than they already have by calling attention to them.

Secondly, it is not a value judgment to describe certain forms as substandard, or not used in more educated circles. It is merely stating a fact and offering a point of valuable information. Labeling a form "substandard" does not mean that the reader may not use it under penalty of the law, or that he may not use it with tongue in cheek, or to produce a certain effect. The educated speaker may want to know what his less fortunate fellow citizens are saying, even without being tempted to imitate them.

Lastly, we cannot altogether go along with the proposition that because language has been allowed to do what it chose in the past it must be allowed to continue to do so in the future. In our twentieth century, we try to control everything. Why not control language, which plays such an important part in our daily lives? Why must it be allowed to lead a life of no restraints, when nobody and nothing else does? If we can intelligently channel it into directions where it will be more expressive, precise, efficient, comprehensible, in short, a better tool of mass communication, why must we assume a passive attitude?

"Usage" sounds good, but whose is the usage? That of those who know how to use usage, or that of those who don't? For language, too, is a skill. We don't allow reckless driving. Why must we allow reckless language?

It may be splitting hairs, in this day and age, to insist upon too fine a distinction between "shall" and "will" (even

Fowler assures us that only southern Englishmen really know how to use those two auxiliaries, and in general speech, after pronouns, both are replaced by " 'll," anyway). But is it really immaterial to merge "uninterested" and "disinterested," in view of their different semantics? "It's me" (or "it's him," for that matter), "Who did you see?" leave the message perfectly clear. Can the same be said of failing to distinguish between "among" and "between," when a court decision hangs on the precise interpretation of an estate to be divided equally "between" two heirs and their issue?

§   §   §

Perhaps I am too visually minded, but there are pronunciations that set my teeth on edge. No matter what the pull of analogy may be, or how exalted the station of the speaker, I cannot bring myself to accept "nucular" for "nuclear" (even Webster's labels it "substandard," thereby attesting its retention of certain standards, as well as its absolute impartiality in the political field).

I find it difficult to swallow "Febuary" for "February" in the otherwise faultless diction of one of our most popular and cultivated TV newscasters. That I am far from alone in my reaction is evidenced by his own admission of protests that have poured in to him. Yet Webster 3 gives "Febuary" as a fully legitimate pronunciation. Advocates of usage remind us of the earlier example of the same phenomenon of dissimilation (*februarius* to *février, febrero, febbraio*, etc.). All the modern Romance languages show the loss of the first of the two *u*'s in the Latin word, just as "Febuary" shows the loss of the first of the two *r*'s in the English. My reply is that the first change took place at a time when literary and educational standards had sunk to an all-time low because the Roman Empire was collapsing. Is "Febuary" an indication that our own "Empire of the Mind" is falling apart? Probus, a third-century A.D. counterpart of mine, carried on his campaign on behalf of the first *u* in *februarius*, but in vain.

Mine, too, may be in vain; at any rate, let it go into the records so that the excavators of our ruins in the year 4000 may read it.

I object (and here I fear I stand almost alone) to the current pronunciation "marjarine" for "margarine," for which there is no justification of spelling, etymology, derivation, or convenience of pronunciation. Why and how it crept in is a mystery. My own guess (but it's only a guess) is that there was analogical influence from the proper name Marjorie. If we must have it (and Webster 3 says we must), can't we at least change the spelling from *g* to *j*? The vagaries of English spelling are numerous and varied, but this seems to be the only sample of *g* before *a* being pronounced as *j*, if we except that British anachronism, *gaol* for *jail*.

I also object to the spoken-language use of "censor" for "censure," as demonstrated by William Miller in his acceptance speech at the 1964 Republican Convention, but sanctioned by Webster 3, though with a mild "chiefly substandard." "Presumptious" for "presumptuous," not mentioned by Webster but used by Senator Kenneth Keating on TV, also wins my condemnation, for what it may be worth.

§   §   §

Jacques Barzun, in his *The House of Intellect,* offers a long list of atrocities culled from the writings of the supposedly educated. Many of them are in the nature of nonce-errors, and reflect nothing but personal ignorance or, at best, mental confusion of one individual ("forced to eat humble crow"; "I am in the throngs of packing"; "they began to strangle in"; "step up on the roster"). A *hapax legomenon* of this type would naturally not be listed in any dictionary. "Self-indulgement" is not reported in Webster 3. Neither is the use of "transportation" in the sense of "railroad ticket," taken from a railroad's announcement ("Luncheon now being served in the dining-car. Take your transportation with you.") This, it seems to us, would be a good subject for inclusion in a comprehensive dictionary of usage, since the usage appears even in recorded written form. On the other hand, Webster 3 gives us as legitimate several forms to which Barzun objects: "panel discussant," "differ with" and "differ from," "quadrimester" in the sense of one of the three terms into which an educational institution subdivides its school year, even though each quadrimester is only three months. "Mixgivings" is, of course, a case of downright mental mixup, and no one would expect to find it, even in Webster 3.

From the abdication of Webster as the Voice of Authority one good result stands out. Editors and publishers who have based their styling, spelling, and punctuation on the usage prescribed by former editions will now have to go easy on the personal preferences of their authors. I have never been able to see, for instance, why a comma or period should be enclosed within a quotation when it logically belongs outside; or why I should not exercise my own discretion as to the use of hyphens, or running words into each other ("mainstream" or "main stream"? "nonconformist" or "non-conformist"?).

For years I have fought my own running battle against American misspellings and mispronunciations of words and names borrowed from other languages, no matter how much sanctioned by Webster's. In the case of family names, if their owners wish to distort them for the sake of making them more accessible to Anglo-Saxon speakers, that is their own affair. This has happened with such names as *Es*-PO-*si-to*, PE-*co-ra*, *Ji*-ME-*nez*, commonly mispronounced, even by their possessors, as *Es-po*-SI-*to*, *Pe*-KO-*ra*, JI-*me-nez*. It has happened with Don Ameche (Amici), who had the surprise of hearing his name pronounced *a*-ME-*ke*, after its new spelling, when he went to Italy. Just to prove I'm neutral, I protested with equal loudness about the Italian rendering of Nicholas Murray Butler as *Nee-koh*-LAHS *Moor*-EYE *Boot*-LEHR.

But I cannot accede to the misspelling of a first name *Giuseppe* as *Guiseppe* (how would one pronounce the name as misspelt, anyway? *guy*-SEP-*pea?*), or to the pronunciation *Cris-to*-FO-*ro* for *cris*-TO-*fo-ro,* or *Bonn Amy* for *Bon Ami.*

§   §   §

Bergen Evans, Apostle of Usage, deplores what he calls "Intimidated English," the sort of "mistake" (I hesitate to use the word in the same breath with Bergen Evans) that people make because they are afraid of falling into the opposite error. Linguists call this "overcorrection," and some among them even resort to a German term, *Umgekehrte Schreibung,* or reverse writing, to denote its written manifestation. This occurs when one says, as frequently happens, "between you and I." Here the mental process runs this way: the speaker is painfully aware of his proneness to use the "incorrect" "it is me" instead of the "correct" "it is I," so he carries the process of correction farther than he should and uses a nominative form after a preposition. Other examples offered by Dr. Evans are "He gave it to John and myself" (where the noncommittal "myself" solves the difficulty of the choice between "me" and "I"); "he's doing finely" (adverbs normally end in -*ly*); "Whom shall I say is calling?" (this overcorrects "Who did you see?"). Such forms crop up where you least expect them. Senator Goldwater, if correctly quoted in *The New York Times,* pledged support before the convention to the Republican Party's nominee, "whomever it might be." For this he has Webster backing, though the phrase is not quite the same.

But there are other constructions, favored by all political parties, which are becoming more and more widespread, and still go unreported by Webster's. Once upon a time, we used to say "so far as something is concerned." The present tendency is to be elliptical and omit the concern. Again if correctly quoted, John F. Kennedy once came out with "So far as the next program, it will be developed later."

Usage and Webster's both sanction such adjectives and participles as "best," "great," "married" in a noun function with an -*s* plural ("the screen bests of 1963"; "the greats of the musical world"; "a couple of young marrieds"). Somehow, these make my hackles rise. So does "teen-aged" for "teen-age" as an adjective, sanctioned by Webster 3.

Another usage I find objectionable, and on which Webster's has nothing to say, is the extremely widespread repetition, both in speech and in writing, of the conjunction "that." Here is a sample culled from the editorial column of my own local newspaper, the *Newark Star-Ledger* (January 31, 1964): "It is ironic *that* in this new period of relaxed tensions *that* an unarmed plane was callously shot down." Can we do something about this? Conversely, if we wish to admit it as "regular" on grounds of widespread use, could Webster 4 make provision for it? It is unjust to ignore it. Still another of my objections is to "these kind of cases," used by J. Edgar Hoover on TV, and about which Webster 3 again seems to have nothing to say.

Lastly, there is an entire series of misspellings (if we may be allowed the term) that creep wholesale into newspaper columns, literary magazines, books, and letters written by literate people. Some are sanctioned by Webster 3, others go unmentioned. Among the latter are some mentioned in Chapter 13 (*seige* for *siege, interchange* of *marital* and *martial,* and so on). In *principle* versus *principal,* the ear deceives the eye, but it shouldn't, since each word has its own clearly defined sphere of action and meaning. Ought not Webster 4 to make some mention of these forms?

Webster 3 does recognize the widespread interchange of the suffixes *-able* and *-ible* (*admissable, permissable,* even *feasable*). This type of error does not occur with high-frequency words, like *possible* and *likable,* which no one dreams of misspelling. Recognition is given to *torturous* for *tortuous,* with a sample from Ralph Ellison; but even if the two words come from the same Latin stem, the semantic difference between torture-giving and winding should be obvious.

The extremely widespread confusion of "its" and "it's" has abundant historical justification, for "it's" was the common way of spelling "its" until about 1800. Etymologically, neither form should have an apostrophe, for -s is the mark of the old Anglo-Saxon genitive case, and other Germanic languages use it without the apostrophe. The use of the latter, when it first began in English, led to such peculiar forms as "John his book," on the assumption that something had been left out. Today, however, the two forms have clearly defined separate realms, and it should be easy enough to remember that "it's" should be used only where it may be replaced by "it is."

In view of the fact that a *c* before *e* and an *s* normally represent the same spoken sound, one should find it easy to forgive *supercede, intersede.* Webster 3 permits the first, but not the second. Here we have only etymology to guide us. The *-cede* element comes from a Latin verb meaning to step, while *-sede* means to sit. Literally, *supersede* is to sit above, *intercede* is to step between; but to step above and to sit between sound just as logical for two literary verbs one of which actually means to replace, the other to plead for. And what of *concensus,* appearing on the educational page of *The New York Times* ("The concensus seemed to be that the wrong target was selected")? Here again, etymology might offer justification, even if Webster 3 doesn't, for "community of meaning" and "community based on enumeration" would both make sense in this context.

§   §   §

The foregoing examples could be multiplied, but they would only amount to more of the same thing. The interpretation may be left to the individual reader.

A narrow conclusion would be to the effect that a dictionary that claims to reflect usage should be more extensive, and aim to cover all widespread deviations from the norm, not merely some; secondarily, that nothing would be lost, and much might be gained, if the dictionary, in listing all forms of usage that are truly usage, and not just the expression of the individual's personal whim, ignorance, or mental confusion, were to offer a limited value judgment on the desirability of using each form listed, basing itself not so much on personal preference, prejudice, or emotion as on three factors that can to a large degree be objectively determined.

The three factors are: (a) the use of such forms by writers and speakers generally recognized to be the best in the field of writing and speaking, rather than in such unrelated activities as politics or sports; (b) the etymological and historical form and meaning of the word; (c) most important of all, the "functional yield" of the word or form in establishing necessary or desirable distinctions of meaning that will make the language more precise and less haphazard. Surely these are goals that are not merely esthetically, sociologically, and economically, but even scientifically worth while.

PART FOUR

a b c d e f g h i j k l m n o p q r s t u v w x y z

WHAT WE DO TO OTHERS

THE FOLLOWING CHAPTERS ARE AN ATTEMPT TO *describe and evaluate the impact of English upon a number of foreign languages since the end of World War II. They form a suitable prelude for the final section of the book, illustrating the power of penetration of our tongue, which in the final analysis may be the yardstick by which English as an international, world-wide language will be measured.*

Chapter 17 was the outcome of a rather extensive survey, done in 1950 with the collaboration of numerous G.I.'s and officers stationed abroad. It is therefore the fruit of firsthand observation, and reflects linguistic conditions in the immediate postwar period. It drew a full-page review-comment in the Moscow Literaturnaya Gazeta, *which was partly critical, partly laudatory. The Russian reviewer was at pains to point to the lack of permanence in English influence on the various vocabularies, with the corollary that our general influence upon the occupied countries was of a highly transitory nature, and that the return of peacetime conditions to Europe and Asia would almost surely see the waning of our international prestige in many fields, that of language included.*

Almost at the same time, however, came a volume prepared by two of Italy's foremost linguists, which presented a quite different picture, as I indicate, with features that had all the earmarks of permanency.

Much more recent is Etiemble's Franglais *of 1964, which paints a devastating portrait of the ravages the French language has undergone in the last decade at the hands of its rival and competitor for the world scene. The fact that Etiemble is violently condemnatory in his attitude toward all forms of Anglo-American influence upon French life and customs should not blind us to the linguistic significance of his work. Milder pronouncements from Italian sources and an echo of Etiemble's alarm voiced by the custodians of the Spanish language only reveal that the influence of English upon the other great lan-*

guages of Western civilization is world-wide and extensive, penetrating in depth at the same time that it spreads out like oil upon the waters.

What all this may portend is perhaps a matter of guesswork. Placed in juxtaposition with Part Five, which shows what is happening in some ultra-modern fields, it may perhaps point to the shape of the International English to come, which seems already to be taking its place, rightful or not, in the world.

CHAPTER SEVENTEEN

A B C D E F G H I J K L M N O P Q R S T U V W X Y Z

G.I. English— Not for Export

Since the war, linguistic authorities have busied themselves with a challenging question: Has G.I. English had any permanent effect on countries visited or occupied by our troops? Although no definite conclusions have been reached, the following survey illustrates the impact of the rich and colorful American language in Europe and Asia.

BRITISH COMMONWEALTH

Has the interchange between British and American English been noticeably speeded by the G.I.'s stationed in England, Australia, and other Commonwealth countries?

The answer is given in a statement by Eric Partridge.

probably the greatest living authority on English slang:
"The language of the G.I.'s has exercised remarkably little
influence either upon Standard English or upon English (or
indeed British) slang. Only two words have gained a general
currency: 'G.I.' itself, and 'jeep.' The main reasons for this
paucity are two: (1) British soldiers have never lacked the
ability to strike a line of their own; (2) the U.S.A. did not
declare war until December 1941; very few American soldiers
were seen in Britain until May 1943; and the contacts in the
Pacific only a very little influenced the Australians and the
New Zealanders (very independent fellows, both of them)."

During the North African campaign, the Americans
agreed to accept *lorry* for *truck* if the British would use *gas*
for *petrol*. But the fact remains that today Americans continue to use *truck* and *gas*, Britishers *lorry* and *petrol*. Those
terms, and many similar ones, are mutually comprehensible,
but hardly interchangeable. What true interchange there is
seems due far more to the influence of the movies, the radio,
the theater, and the press, than to any colloquial G.I. influx.

GERMANY

The director of the Army Education Center in Frankfurt
denied that the German language has been heavily infil-
trated by G.I. English, since most communication between
the American soldiers and the German populace is carried
on by means of G.I. German, the Americans speaking German without regard for inflections or grammatical gender.

Copious examples contradict this viewpoint. Not only
expressions like *O.K., jeep, Coca Cola, nylon* (*ein Paar
Nylons*) have penetrated the current German language, but
also terms like *snack bar, ice cream* (more commonly spelled
ice creme, and kept distinct from the native German *Eis*),
sandwich, doughnuts, party (in the festive, not the political
sense), *drink* (*ich möchte ein Drink haben*). For some (not
all) of these terms it might be argued that the object the

name stands for had not previously existed in the country, so that the Germans borrowed *snack bar* from American English much as the Americans had previously borrowed *spaghetti* from Italian. But *frankfurter* and *hamburger,* also adopted by German, were formerly precisely represented in German by *Wiener Wurst* and *Fleischpflanzchen* (or *deutsches Beefsteak*). A philologist would point out that the frankfurter and hamburger were once of German origin, so that they are in the nature of birds coming home to roost.

A small army of what linguists call loan translations have penetrated the German language. G.I. "to be fixin' to do something" has influenced present-day German *Ich muss es fixen* (instead of the legitimate *reparieren*); "to give someone a hard time" comes out literally: *er hat mir eine harte Zeit gegeben.* "Come on, let's go!" is not even translated when it is used, but *chewing gum* is; *ein Kaugummi Arbeiter* is a slow worker. Girls who fraternize with American soldiers are known as *Coca Cola Fräulein, Flaschen Baby,* or *Blondie.* For *es macht nichts* ("it doesn't matter," "never mind") many Germans have adopted the American pronunciation, *maax nix.* As a derogatory term, they have borrowed *Kraut* from the Americans. Lovely samples of double borrowing are the French *beaucoup* and *comme ci, comme ça,* brought into Germany by the G.I.'s, then appropriated by the Germans (*geben Sie mir beaucoup Bier; wie haben Sie es bekommen? Comme ci, comme ça,* usually accompanied by a gesture that indicates swiping).

There is some doubt whether the change in the German way of compounding numerals (*zwanzig-ein, zwanzig-zwei,* twenty-one, twenty-two, for the older *ein und zwanzig, zwei und zwanzig*) is due to military or to cultural influences. Other terms that have penetrated the German language— *team, comeback, boogie woogie, swing, rumba, samba, hillbilly*—can definitely be scored on the non-military side of the ledger.

A few German neologisms due to American military influence, though not directly borrowed from G.I. talk, had been previously noticed by linguists. One was *Luftgangster* (air gangster), the term used by the Nazis to designate our bombing airmen. Another was *Ami-töter,* "American-killer," for the Russian-made cigarette that came into Berlin at the height of the cigarette black-market activities, and broke the American monopoly on the medium of exchange (the Russians' own name for their cigarette was *Drug,* friend). The abbreviation U.S.A., interpreted by some Nazi diehards as *unser seeliger Adolf,* is a good sample of borrowing accompanied by distortion of meaning.

FRANCE

France is a hospitable land, linguistically as well as politically. Unlike the stiff-necked Germans, the French take spontaneously, even eagerly, to linguistic innovations from other lands. In the past, and under the most diverse circumstances, French has adopted such English terms as *baby, bridge, club, film, sandwich, wagon, smoking, boxe,* and *bouledogue.* A popular French cigarette of the first decade of the century was called *High-Life* (pronounced, however, *Heeg-Leaf*).

The following expressions are all currently accepted and understood in France: *Le Jitter-bug en trois Leçons* (jitterbugging in three lessons); *Superfemme* (a lightly clad comicstrip character whose relationship to Superman is obvious); *gangster, gangsterisme, gangster girls; steak* (for the older loan word *bifteck*); *des shorts; le be-bop; le pays du cocacola; un bikini; starlette; technicolor; boyfriend* (spelled as one word); *dynamique; il avait des yeux swing* ("he had swing eyes"; new usage of a familiar word); *les capitales européennes connectées entre elles* (good French except for *connectées*); *new look* (more commonly spelled *nioulouque* or *néolouque*); *bestseller; groggy; racket; covergirl;* plus an entire series of baseball terms: *baseballeur, lanceur, attrapeur* (literal translation of pitcher and catcher); *petit et grand champ* (infield and outfield); *bonne et mauvaise* (fair and foul); *tuez l'arbitre* (kill the umpire).

Any or all of these expressions could conceivably have come from the G.I.'s, but how to prove it? A better case could perhaps be built for military expressions like *le radar* and *le fuel*. Knowledge of G.I. habits casts the spotlight of strong suspicion upon *les pin-up girls de la belle France; le gang des pin-ups; elle est très pin-up* (she is very pin-up; again a case where French carries the expression farther than English). Even more suspicious sounding is *un jeu de craps accompagné de jurons américanisés* (a game of craps accompanied by Americanized cuss words). We have, fortunately, definite proof in a French phrasebook for G.I.'s that the pronunciation *Reems* for the city of Rheims (in authentic French it would sound somewhat like *Rance*) was devised during the war by French train conductors for the guidance of our soldiers, but its postwar survival is extremely doubtful. The naming of streets and avenues after American fighting units, like Metz's *Avenue du Twentieth American Army Corps,* is a phenomenon that dates back to World War I, but it can hardly be accepted as a penetration of the popular language.

All these terms represent slim pickings when compared with the many expressions the French borrowed from G.I.'s of other lands during former occupations of their territory: the Russian *bistro* (quick, fast) to denote a low drinking dive; the Croatian-derived *cravate,* or neckscarf, worn by Austrian cavalrymen in the days of Napoleon's downfall; the *vasistas* which represents German *Was ist das?* (What is that?), applied to a transom which occupying German troops admired for the first time on French soil; perhaps also *kaput* (finished, dead); *pumpernickel,* which the French etymologize, rightly or wrongly, as *bon pour Nickel* ("good for Nickel," the dog); possibly even *choucroute,* which is the last part of German *Sauerkraut* with the French word for "cabbage" prefixed, making "cabbage-cabbage" out of the mess.

If the French did not pick up more G.I. English, it certainly was not our government's fault. During the war, I helped to construct for the Office of War Information a dictionary and phrase book of G.I. English for the use of French speakers, with phonetic transcriptions such as SOL-*djeur* for soldier. But so far as I am able to ascertain, not a single one of my words and phrases survives in *le français d'aujourd'hui.*

ITALY

Here it must not be forgotten that American influence was quite strong even before the war, not only in literary, sporting, or amusement circles, as in France, but in the homey, earthy language of the masses. The town of Ricigliano, in the province of Salerno, used *O.K.* long before the first G.I. set foot on Italian soil, since three fourths of its population had been to the United States and had returned home with a Chicago Midwestern accent. The really popular language of Ponza, a small island near Naples with about eight thousand inhabitants, was Brooklynese, for the same reason. Hybrid expressions like *una boxa di mecci* ("a box of matches"; good Italian would be *una scatola di fiammiferi*), or *nu bellu cottu* ("a fine coat," in the place of standard Italian *un bel soprabito*) could occasionally be heard on Italian soil.

Nevertheless, the impact of G.I. English on Italian is both considerable and sharply defined, as testified by this report from an American army major of Italian descent, a former student of linguistics at Columbia, and later director of the United States Information Service for southern Italy (still later he was American Consul General in half a dozen assorted countries; now he is "retired" as head of the languages department at Moorhead State College in Minnesota):

> I feel certain that the hundreds of thousands of boys who spent so much time in Italy will be rather proud of their knowledge of Italian, and will be eager, many of them, to solidify what they learned. The great majority are still,

of course, at the stage where all Italian verbs exist only in the infinitive, and it's a source of delight to me to note how strong *our* influence has been on the Italians. All the shopkeepers, all the *donnine,* all the *sciuscià* (bootblacks) have evolved their own pidgin, and get along swimmingly with the G.I.'s. It has reached the point where now it's almost useless to try to speak Italian to the small tradesmen. The *cameriera* will say: *"Lei dare me two stecche ciuinga, io fare biancheria voi subito."* The *portiere* invariably says: *"Dove andare?"* if you go past him without stating whom you're visiting. To hear a soldier address a *signorina* (whom he invariably calls a *señorita*) is a treat. He will probably reply to her "Shack job, Joe?" with *"Io no avere molto lire. Quanto costare voi?"* The reply is usually something like 5,000 lire, with lots of takers. Even the *ruffiani* (pimps) use the word *señorita* now. I suppose it's the standard form in the Army, because the boys used the term in North Africa, where it took hold. Oddly enough, the word *vino* instead of *vin* became the accepted form in Africa, too, long before any of the boys had gone to Sicily. Influence of the movies? Or our fellows from the Southwest? Or the great many Italo-Americans whose little knowledge of Italian made them interpreters for their fellows in Algiers and Tunisia? Anyway, you will see how very well a great many of the G.I.'s learned to speak languages other than their own. I've heard some excellent Sicilian spoken by an army officer who had never been out of Wisconsin, but who had to learn it in a town in Trapani province. And others whose Arabic was perfectly intelligible to the Arabs. And now they are meeting Romans and Florentines and Bolognesi. Our American officers of Italian descent who claimed to speak Italian, but spoke only that compound of Neapolitan–Abruzzese–Barese–Sicilian–Calabrian that passes for Italian in New York are finding the going rugged, and have had to work hard to catch up with the officers who weren't under that handicap.

As to the converse Italian borrowings from G.I. English, the form *okeyna* was used during the war by the Italians to denote a girl who fraternized too freely with the invaders.

Vacca (literally cow) for WAC caused much laughter, but did not last long. *Señorita* and *signorina* were finally blended into *segnorina*. G.I.'s who really knew Italian and tried to use the inflected form of the verb instead of the universalized infinitive were actually "corrected" by Italian speakers who had acquired the infinitive habit.

Names of American products have become extremely common, but it is difficult to prove that they were introduced by the G.I.'s; there is *Lux,* for instance, and *gomma americana* (bubble gum, as opposed to *ciuinga,* or ordinary chewing gum); and, of course, the universal *Coca-Cola.* Terms like *pulova* (pullover) and *golfino* (cardigan) abound, but evidence of G.I. influence is doubtful. Other popular words are *nailon, colcrem, futbol,* and *skunk* (pronounced skoonk, and applied only to the fur, since the Italian name for the living animal is, appropriately enough, *puzzola,* or stinkie).

An entire series of English borrowings has been reported by the Italian linguist Alberto Menarini. Italian war prisoners in North Africa used *brek, brekkaggio,* and even the verb *brekkare* (from English break), meaning to stop off work. *Spiccare* for to speak (in authentic Italian it means to stand out), and *spiccata* for speech arose, along with *giobbare* (from job) for to work. *Tegedizi* represented the English take it easy, while *kalabush,* taken from a *calaboose* which is itself a southwestern borrowing from Mexican-Spanish *calabozo,* meant jail or jug. *Tumorro* came from English tomorrow, but was used as an adjective in the sense of lazy, slow (*E' il funzionario più tumorro di tutto l'accampamento,* He's the laziest official in the whole camp).

It is not generally known, even by those who saw the film *Paisan,* that this term was the regular southern Italian designation for an American soldier. *Paisa'* (southern dialect for *paesano,* fellow countryman, fellow townsman) was used by Italo-American G.I.'s in their first contacts with the inhabitants of the invaded southern provinces of Italy; and the Italians, who liked the Americans and thought at least half of them were of Italian descent anyway, enthusiastically returned the compliment. Other Italian terms for American soldiers were *Johnny* (or *Gionni*) and *kaman* (from come on).

A wholesale shift in the meanings of certain legitimate Italian words came about by reason of the intrusion of their English cognates. The prewar Italian term for civilian, for example, was *borghese,* from the same root that gives us *bourgeois,* while *civile* was used only as an adjective with the meaning civil or civilized. With the coming of the Americans, *civile* began to take on the meaning of civilian as opposed to military. *Liberazione,* liberation, meant specifically the liberation of Italy from German domination. Postwar terms that bear the stamp of G.I. influence are *riconversione, riabilitazione* (rehabilitation, even in prewar days, but now used with a material and economic rather than a moral connotation), *emergenza* (formerly used in the sense of emergence, now of emergency).

Terms like *sceriffo* were given by Italian partisans as names for jeeps. *Sceriffo* can be found in Italian dictionaries, but is seldom used in the spoken tongue; its original Arabic meaning was Arab chieftain. The partisans' *sceriffo* was obviously borrowed from our western sheriff, which is of Anglo-Saxon, not of Arabic origin. *Buki buki* is American boogie woogie, but G.I. influence, while probable, is difficult to prove. *Gangster* was used indifferently for a jeep or a black-market operator, and the verb *gangsterare* arose to describe the operations of the latter. Terms like *il vecchio* (the old man), applied especially to Mussolini, seem to be loan translations. Conversely, American G.I.'s in Italy were occasionally heard to use *Teds* for the Germans (from Italian *tedesco,* German).

All linguists are agreed that the one German word that gained widest currency in Italy was *kaput,* standing for death or destruction. The most widespread American word is *O.K.,* a cry of optimism, friendliness, and encouragement.

JAPAN

Japanese admiration for America and things American goes all the way back to Commodore Perry and the middle of the nineteenth century. The Japanese loved us even while they hated us, and neglected no opportunity to imitate us. The prewar Japanese language is full of English words, some of which came from the British, but most of which were contributed by us. All are subject to the Japanese sound system, whereby *r* replaces *l*, no words end in consonants (save *n*), and vowels must be inserted between two different consonant sounds. Our gasoline has become their *gasorin* (note that it was the American gasoline, not the British petrol, that was borrowed). Our pound is their *pondo*, our tip their *chippu*. The two Japanese loan words for dollar, *doru* and *dara*, reflect respectively British and American pronunciation. When the Japanese began using Western-style foods, they borrowed the names with the objects: *bifuteki, choppu, bata, soppu, hamu, beikon, chiizu, sarada. Soseiji* is sausage, *biru* is beer, *kōhī* is coffee, *remon* is lemon. *Wisuki* should be self-explanatory. Even Western tableware was included, as witnessed by *naifu, fōku, nafukin*. Architectural terms like *birujingu* (building), *hoteru, suteishon* (station), *purattohōmu* (this is as close as Japanese phonology can get to platform); household terms like *teiburu* (table), *matoresu, rampu* (lamp); conveyances like *takushi* and *basu* (bus); clothing items like *shatsu* (shirt), *kara* (collar), *nekutai, hankechi, botan, pin, surippa* (slipper); general utility articles like *toranku* (trunk), *pen* and *inki, maki-tabako* (cigarette) and *matchi;* names of amusements, like *dansu* and *pikunikku,* all came to the Japanese from us in pre-Pearl Harbor days, along with a wholesale baseball terminology and quite a few military and naval terms.

During the war, half-hearted attempts were made to eradicate English words from the Japanese vocabulary, but it was already too late. The penetration had gone too far. With the American occupation, the Japanese returned enthusiastically to their American vocabulary, and added to it mightily.

Such words as *jipu* (jeep), *gasu* (gas), *chuing gommo, herro* and *goombai* (hello and good-bye), *O Kei* have joined the long list of their predecessors. So likewise a new list of American products: *sigaretto, chokoretto* (two black-market staples), *koka-kora* and its competitor *pepusi-kora, kanu* (from can, but used in connection with C-rations), *miruku* and *keiki* (milk and cake); the use of English military titles like Captain, Lieutenant, Major (commonly replaced by the Japanese equivalent *tai* when the person addressed knows Japanese); the use of a person's first name, as in American familiar address, but with the polite Japanese *san* placed after it; *yami soba,* or black market, shortened to *yami* in accordance with one approved feature of American linguistic procedure (*mike* for microphone, *vet* for veteran or veterinary, *doc* for doctor, etc.).

A long list of American improprieties and obscenities has become current in Japan by reason of G.I. influence: words like *basutadu* and *sutinka,* to cite some of the milder forms, or an unexplained *sukipi* (skippy) for sexual intercourse. The G.I. idea of a good joke was to instruct Japanese waitresses and chambermaids that all Americans must be addressed as "son-of-a-bitch *san,*" and these directions were duly followed, with what results one can imagine.

The Japanese greeting *ohayō* was shortened to the middle syllable, to sound exactly like the G.I. "Hi!" *Hubba hubba* (itself a mysterious expression, which some G.I.'s like to derive from Arabic *merhaba,* a form of polite greeting) was transmitted to the Japanese as an adverb meaning fast, quickly ("You want I clean room hubba hubba?"). It is probably the most extensively adopted single American expression used regularly by the Japanese among themselves (*Ikimashō hubba hubba!,* Let's go quick!).

It would indeed be a feather in the G.I.'s cap if this ditty, currently sung in Tokyo, could be attributed to him.

"Buddha loves me, this I know, 'Cause the Sutras tell me so." Missionary influence seems much safer and surer, however, with Buddha and the Sutras replacing Jesus and the Bible.

OTHER COUNTRIES

In the Solomon Islands the native Melanesian Pidgin English lacked many forms which the American troops supplied. Dollars had never been heard of before the war, but by its close all natives knew that word and its significance. An American major stationed in the Solomons comments that the natives, accustomed to English silver coins, were at first suspicious of paper dollars. They insisted to the end on being paid in one-dollar bills rather than in larger denominations. "Truck" was another American term and institution, all previous transportation having been accomplished by handpower. Indeed, the natives embarrassed the English copra traders no end after the Americans were gone by asking: "Master, where truck?"

In China, the designation for an American jeep was rendered by words and written characters having the literal meaning of "little tough guy," while Coca Cola became "make man mouth happy." Previously, the Chinese had borrowed such words as *yu meh* (English humor), *p'u k'e* (poker), *te lu fêng* (telephone). But China, like Germany, seems to have been too proud of her native culture to borrow very extensively from American sources.

Postwar Russia uses the term *amerikanka* (literally, American woman) for beauty shop, but G.I. influence is almost as doubtful as in the case of prewar French *vol à l'américaine* (American theft, confidence game), Italian *American Bar* (soft drink bar) or *americano al selz* (vermouth and soda), Turkish *American bird* (turkey), or Portuguese *um americano* (a streetcar).

There is, of course, an equal or even more extensive

vocabulary of French, German, Italian, Japanese, and other terms acquired by G.I.'s and just as promptly discarded on their return home. French *zig-zig*, Italian *fig-fig*, Filipino *pan-pan* for sexual intercourse; Chinese *gung ho* (all together) and *ding hao* (O.K.), Japanese *ano ne* (hey there!), *ichi, ni, san* (one, two, three); *so desu ka* (izzatso?), *wakarimasen* (I don't understand), *arigatō* (thanks), *dō itashimash'ta* (don't mention it), *dōzo* (please); or mixed terms like *mizu, pleezu* (water, please).

§   §   §

The comparatively short duration of the American occupation and its temporary character, even where it still endures, are generally responsible for the relative paucity of borrowings. Were the G.I. occupation of foreign countries to share the features of permanency that characterized the Roman seizure of Gaul and Iberia, or the Spanish occupation of Central and South America, the story would be different. Above all, were it to extend over centuries instead of years, we would have the emergence of mixed languages, or the triumph of English over the native tongues. It must not be forgotten that for centuries after the Romans occupied Iberia and Gaul the natives continued to speak Iberian and Gaulish, and that the process of Romanization was not completed until the Empire was moving toward its downfall. In Mexico and South America there are yet today, four centuries after the Spanish conquest, large areas in which the native Indian languages still hold undisputed sway, and Spanish is practically a foreign tongue.

Again, our G.I's were up against established, cultured, and cultural national tongues, unlike the Romans and the Spaniards, who found themselves in a position of absolute cultural superiority with respect to the subjugated tribes. A language that is the vehicle of a rich, deeply rooted national civilization will borrow from another tongue with which it comes in contact, but it will be selective rather than indiscriminate borrowing. This is particularly evident in the case of French, which has predominantly borrowed not from lowly G.I. talk, but from our pre- and postwar vocabulary of sports, amusements, and journalism.

The nature of the words borrowed is revealing. Our G.I's were drawn from all walks of life, but for that very reason their linguistic least common denominator was low. This meant that extremely popular words and phrases, commonplaces and improprieties, had a better chance of being heard and borrowed than the more elevated portion of our vocabulary. *O.K.* was used by literally every one in the Armed Services; accordingly, *O.K.* is to be found at or near the top of the list in every country of occupation. Ease of pronunciation may have had something to do with *O.K's* triumph, too. It fits easily into the phonetic pattern of German, French, Italian, Japanese, Chinese, and practically any other language.

But all this does not explain the discrepancy between one foreign tongue and another, the free-and-easy Japanese acceptance of all sorts of G.I. terms and phrases as contrasted with the stubborn British refusal to have any part of G.I. English, the rather limited borrowing of German and the delicate pickiness and choosiness of French against the hearty acceptance of Italian. Here, I suspect, is an expression of the imponderable something which the French call the "genius" of the language, coupled with the disposition of its speakers under a special set of circumstances.

To the British, we were still "colonials," and as such, unworthy of linguistic imitation. The Germans probably consider our cultural patterns too weak and shallow to allow them to do more than dent the walls of their Teutonic *Kultur.* To the Japanese, on the other hand, we were the nation that had first brought them the light of Western progress, the originators of the baseball which they love fully as much as we do, the dwellers in that fabulous land of wealth and plenty which they call *Bei koku,* or rice-land, whom they wished down in the bottom of their hearts not to destroy, but to imitate. What was more natural than that they should pick all they could from our men, even to the language?

The French like us well enough, but they definitely consider themselves culturally superior. To them, Americans are good people, but uncouth; where they imitate us, they do it with tongue in cheek, and with a distinct understanding that it is something in the nature of a prank; hence the appropriation of such terms as *pin-up, craps, boyfriend, starlette, swing,* coupled with a general eschewing of the more rough-and-tumble G.I. phraseology. The Italians were perhaps the people best attuned to our tempo. They knew us from before with our shortcomings, which they easily forgave, and our virtues, which were enhanced in their eyes by the glowing descriptions sent home by their emigrant kinsmen. One tenth of our G.I.'s, roughly, were of Italian descent, and—unlike our soldiers of German ancestry— they were only one or two generations removed from their Italian heritage. There was, consequently, an immediate meeting of minds, hearts, and tongues.

The lesson of G.I. English and its impact upon foreign languages is one to be pondered. Material conquest and occupation do not suffice to bring about linguistic blending. It is only when there is mutual understanding, liking, and (strange as the term may sound in this connection) respect, that words and forms are borrowed and exchanged. The workings of G.I. English in foreign lands may yet lead to a new interpretation of the great historical linguistic transformations whereby the Mediterranean world of antiquity became Latin-speaking under the Romans, but failed to turn Teutonic-speaking with the Germanic invasions, and Latin America relinquished its ancestral Indian languages in favor of Spanish and Portuguese. They may also point to a pattern for the future, if one of the existing national languages, like English or Russian, is eventually to emerge as the universal tongue of mankind.

What We Have Done to One Language

To see ourselves as others see us is sometimes a blessing. Linguistically, it is of help to go through an up-to-date dictionary of a foreign language and see which of our numerous words have traveled abroad, and in what fashion.

Panzini's *Dizionario Moderno* (with Foreword by A. Schiaffini), work on which began as long ago as 1890, with the first edition appearing in 1905, is now in its ninth, 1950 edition, with a brand-new 8,000-word Appendix by Bruno Migliorini. It is this Appendix in particular that will interest students of the English language, since it contains many English words, the majority of them from American English, which have penetrated Italian in recent years, as a result of G.I. permanence in Italy and of what the Reds like to refer to as our "imperialistic commercial and cultural dominance" over the country.

Not that Panzini's own work is free from English importations. Quite the contrary. But while the average is about one English word per page in his section of the work, it often runs up to six or seven words per page in the Appendix.

The varying fortune of words is strikingly illustrated in these loans. We find cases of words transferred from one language to the other without any change of form or meaning (*Babbitt, homemade, jazz band, kodak, knockout, nylon, weekend*); words which have undergone peculiar transformations in the course of their migration (*andicappare,* which is handicap used as a vcrb; or *blackbouler,* to blackball, which is the French form given to the English word, then passed on without further change to Italian); words and expressions in which the British acceptance prevails (*railway,* but not *railroad*), and others in which American usage triumphs (*hoarding,* not as billboard, but as "the stowing away of things for future use"). There are words which come from the language of Italian laborers in America (*boss*); others which those laborers coined for themselves on the basis of an existing English word (*bordo* in the sense of boardinghouse; *giobbo* for job; *ticchetto* for ticket); others again which appear in English form side by side with an Italianized form (*boy scout,* or, somewhat humorously, *biscotto,* which is traditional Italian for cracker); and a few in which the English meaning is erroneously interpreted—*bluff,* for instance, appears in Italian in the same sense as bluff at poker, but the original English meaning is given as "gust of wind," a usage I have not been able to trace in the English dictionaries at my disposal; or *keep your schoolgirl complexion,* in which *complexion,* by semantic misinterpretation, is given as *figurino,* Italian for outline, silhouette; curiously, this error is repeated later by Migliorini, who translates *complexion* by *complessione, corporatura,* both of which mean body build, instead of by the semantically correct *carnagione.*

Panzini's portion of the book was completed in 1939, when relations between America and Mussolini's Italy were strained; it is therefore not surprising to find a few unfavorable allusions to American customs. *Americanata* is defined as "an amazing, daring feat or enterprise, brazen in its use of advertising"; one of the meanings given *americanismo* is "excessive admiration for or imitation of the moral or practical customs of the Americans." For *wilsonismo* we find "originally, an ideal of human betterment; later, when the idol fell, Messianic spirit, utopianism, or even business spirit masked with ideals." *Jazz band* is described as "the name of an orchestra imported from America, for savage dances among civilized people," while *swing* is "an exasperated form of jazz."

By way of contrast, Migliorini's Appendix is highly non-committal and free from subjective judgments, as one might well expect in these days of Western cooperation and an Atlantic Pact. It is also extremely accurate.

One is amazed at the number and variety of Anglo-American words and expressions that appear in the Italian of 1950. One would expect, from war experience, such words as *bazooka, G.I., jeep* (more commonly spelled *gip*), *bulldozer, liberare, pin-up girl, sonar, radar, loran, scrip, Spitfire, Liberatore, Constellation,* even *crap, darling, dear,* and *date*. Political events before and since the war have contributed, logically enough, expressions like *appeasement, atomica, cash and carry, caucus, dogoodism, dollar diplomacy, marshalliano, Solid South, perdere l'autobus* (to miss the bus). Our entertainment industries are responsible for such Italian innovations as *ballyhoo, bebop, best seller* (over-precisely defined, however, as "a book whose sale surpasses one per cent of the population of the continental United States within ten years of publication"), *boogie woogie, burlesque, gagman, ganghista, gangsterare* (but this means "to gouge on the black market," so far as Italy is concerned), *gossip writer, hot, juke box, nastro comico* (this is literal for comic strip; *fumetto,* little smoke, applied to quotations of comic-strip characters, is just as often used for the entire strip); *nemico pubblico numero uno, Pathé baby, preview, ragtime, recital, silly symphony, scoop, soap opera, spiritual, stand-in, thrilling,* and *capelli alla Ty* (defined as hair parted on the side, Tyrone Power style).

The changing semantics of words is illustrated by *clergyman,* defined as the black habit with closed collar worn by Catholic priests in the United States; *corned beef,* which in Italy, according to the definition, can be obtained only in canned form; *groggy,* which is rendered by the Italian equivalent for knocked out; *kid* and *lad,* the first of which is defined as simply a prize-fighting nickname, while the second is connected only with horse racing; *quiz,* which is quite overlooked by Italian in its meaning of "informal school exam," and related only to quiz programs; *soda parlor,* which to us is a place where soft drinks are sold, but in Italy appears as a whisky-and-soda dispensary; *Oswego* (or *Osvego*), said to be the name of a type of biscuit named after the city of Oswego, New York. *Slum* shows a definite restriction of meaning in its Italian acceptance: "lurid alley," "uninhabitable hut."

Loan translations are common. Among others we find: *obiettore di coscienza* (conscientious objector); *richiamo alla foresta* (call of the wild); *anno sabbatico* (sabbatical year); *trust dei cervelli* (brain trust). *Pizzicare* (literally, to pinch) is used in Italian slang precisely as in our own (to arrest), and one is forced to wonder whether one language did not influence the other, and if so, which had priority.

Words that change their form to conform to the Italian phonemic pattern are many. *Bovindo,* from the Italian standpoint, would seem to be connected with an ox; actually, it is the English *bow window. Impatto, pinnacolo, praticamente,* and *prospettore* are our impact, pinnacle, practically, and prospector (it may be noted that *praticamente* existed in Italian before the days of Anglo-American influence, but only in the sense of "in practical fashion"). *Spiccare,* which in legitimate Italian means "to stand out", is jocularly used for "to speak."

A few points on which I would disagree with Migliorini are: *hellzapoppin'* is not onomatopoetic, but derived from "hell is a-popping"; *high-brow* does not literally mean *altociglio* (*ciglio* is Italian for eyelash, *sopracciglio* for eyebrow, *fronte* for brow or forehead); *ketchup,* which he derives from Chinese, is given by Webster as from Malay; the expression commonly used in the United States is *lend-lease,* not *lend and lease; off limits* is said to be the American locution, *out of bounds* the British; I believe I have heard both in the military parlance of the United States.

There is humor in many of these words. *Mobo* is a Japanese word that has come into Italian; it means a Japanese young man with Western ideas. But where did the Japanese get it? Nowhere else than in the United States; it is an abbreviated *modern boy,* just as *mogaru* is *modern girl.*

Sprinkler to us is a harmless piece of garden equipment; in Italy it is a political weapon—a pump filled with indelible ink which, used by the police while a riot is in progress, permits the rioters to be tracked down later.

The *Dizionario Moderno* gives both the traditional Italian *caffetteria* (café, coffee shop) and the English adaptation *cafeteria,* defined as a United States self-service restaurant; you are then referred to *ciberia,* a coined word the literal equivalent of which would be *foodery.* The coiner is none other than Professor Giuseppe Prezzolini, formerly of Columbia University, who in his writings thus describes the American cafeteria: "one of those places which I would call fooderies (*ciberie*), because they resemble hospitals by reason of their luxurious crockery, and also because they stimulate the appetite about as much as a hospital does."

There is probably one Italian out of a hundred who is familiar with the ancient Italian word for *beeksteak* or *bistecca,* used before the importations from England began. I must confess that I was among the ninety-nine. But now, thanks to *Dizionario Moderno,* I know. The word is *carbonata* (that which is cooked over the coals or embers). But if you travel to Italy I would still hesitate to advise you to ask for a *carbonata;* you had better hang on to *bistecca* or *beefsteak.*

But What Have We Done for Them Lately?

An earlier chapter minimized the impact of English, particularly G.I. English, on French. But that was in 1950. Fourteen years can make a great deal of difference in linguistic history. This was abundantly proved by René Etiemble, the French professor who spent some years during the war teaching at the University of Chicago, did not care much for what he saw there, and migrated back to a liberated Sorbonne in Paris when the war was over. Some of Etiemble's books were published in the United States (his *Orion Book of the Written Word,* published in 1961, enjoyed rather favorable reviews). In 1964, Etiemble came out with a 370-page blast against what he called *le Franglais* ("Atlantic Sabir" is another of his names for it; *Sabir,* derived from Spanish *saber,* to know, and related to English *savvy,* was a term devised by Molière in his *Bourgeois Gentilhomme* to denote the pidgin previously known as lingua franca, a mixture of Italian, Arabic, French, Spanish, Greek, and other Mediterranean tongues, which was used as a language of common intercourse in the entire Mediterranean area during the Middle Ages and the Renaissance; in modern linguistic parlance, Sabir is more or less equated to pidgin). *Franglais,* or *Sabir Atlantique,* is in Etiemble's concept the new, ultra-modern French language, interlarded with Anglo-American words

and expressions, even grammatical and stylistic constructions, which two postwar decades, the Marshall Plan, the
Atlantic Pact, and NATO have produced, in collaboration
with American commercial and cultural penetration of the
lands of Western Europe, and with the connivance of Western
European businessmen, hotel keepers, advertisers, military
men, bureaucrats, and even scholars.

The book is one that no student of contemporary French
can afford to miss. In some ways, it is a book that no American
can afford to miss, because it gives a very clear explanation of the assorted reasons, right or wrong, why we are not
liked abroad, particularly by the people who should feel
most in our debt.

One need not at all agree with Etiemble's distorted point
of view to enjoy the book. Etiemble has been described as
a communist or, at the very least, a communist sympathizer.
There is little in his book that lends itself to this charge.
Had the book been translated into English and widely circu-
lated in the United States, we might have been better prepared for de Gaulle's defection from NATO. It would have
given us some plausible, if not reasonable, explanation of
the grounds for that defection. As matters stand, I would
place Etiemble's book in the same class with Hitler's *Mein
Kampf* and the assorted writings of Marx, Lenin, and Mao
—all works which Americans should have read in order to
understand the precise nature of the ideological forces ar-
rayed against them, but which they have in fact failed to
read.

Etiemble's economic-political strictures are a matter of individual opinion. His linguistic description of what we have
done to the French language is a matter of historical record.

His first three chapters ("Tales which become less and
less funny" as they go) are a series of fictional episodes, of
not too inspiring an order, dealing with the unlikely adventures of imaginary characters. But these characters think,
speak, and live in a linguistic atmosphere that is neither
French nor English, but a mixture of the two. The author

gives us paragraph after paragraph in which the basic structure is French, but the vocabulary, particularly for what
concerns nouns, largely English. A few samples:

§   §   §

*"Je ne suis pas un squatter . . . Je n'habite pas un building
de grand standing; mon home est modeste; ce n'est pas une
pent-house; je ne vous y montrerai pas de game-room; je ne
dispose ni de lift-boy, ni même de lift . . ."*

§   §   §

*Jacqueline la stewardess fouilla dans son sac, en sortit quel-
ques gadgets dont un contraceptive éprouvé, éparpilla sur
le divan deux ou trois compacts et un charmant utility . . .*

§   §   §

*"Tu ne pourrais pas demander à l'un des public-relations
men de ta Compagnie de m'accorder une interview? J'aime-
rais trouver un nouveau job . . ."*

§   §   §

*Tout dans le living-room paraissait confortable: le shaker
sur le bar, le fauteuil club à côté du cosy-corner. Simone,
très sexy dans son blue jeans et son twin set de cashmere
fully fashioned, se remit du compact sur le bout du nez
avant d'enfiler ses snow-boots et son duffle-coat.*

§   §   §

Other chapters are entitled "Baby Corner et Coin des
Teens," "Men's Department," "O'She Club." Throughout
this first section, we are introduced to hundreds, perhaps
thousands, of words and expressions which, according to
Etiemble, have become standard, even elegant French. They
run all the way from the frivolous (*High Society, party, deb,
joke, teenager, play boy, pin-up boy, petting, glamorous,
bobby-soxers, cover girls, call-girls*) to the deadly serious
(*black out, rifle, holster, gun man, muscle man, trigger man,*

kidnapper, underworld); from the utilitarian (*derrick, bull-dozer, pipeline, starter, scooter, roadster, parking, hard-top, jet clipper, non-stop, rush, boom, royalties, business man, full time, part time*) to the pleasurable (*soft drink, ham-burger, hot dog, ketchup, lunch, crackers, goldens, grape-fruits,* even *rumsteak,* whatever that may be); from articles you acquire in a *drugstore* (*cold cream, cleansing cream, kleenex, quickies, long-acting sulfa, Air-wick*) to such assorted items as *motels, bird watchers, girl scouts, come backs,* and *comingmen.*

It may have been noted that when the English form gets into French, it may be given a different word division from the one we customarily employ (*playboy, blackout, gunman, comeback,* for example, would be our preferred forms; we would have *coming man* as two separate words; hyphens are today a matter of opinion, but *grapefruit* would normally lack both the hyphen and the *-s* plural ending in American use).

Etiemble's *Sabir* contains plenty of mixed words, some of which are of very ancient vintage (like *gentleman-cambrioleur;* more recent are *quick lait,* which alternates with the older *milk bar; shopping-libre,* which is our *super-market; self-beauté,* which we suspect is meant to represent our *home permanent*). There are words where French, or even German, supplies the suffix (*starlette, teenette, mo-toriste, stockiste, turfiste;* even *speakerine,* which is a female announcer). There are such loan translations as *argent dur* (hard cash) and *magasin de marchandises sèches* (dry-goods store). *Autostopiste* (hitchhiker) works on an English verb-stem, but is otherwise quite different from our term; we learn from other sources that it appears also in Italian (*autostoppista*). *Breatheliser* is our drunkometer, or drunk-meter, again formed on the stem of an English verb, but otherwise unknown to Americans. *Karting* is some sort of sport or game, attributed to us. *Happy end* takes the place of our *happy ending* in films and stories. *Crack* is also spelled *krach,* and is used in Etiemble's episodes to refer both to the Wall Street collapse of 1929 (*crack* was used to denote a business or stock market *crash* in many continental languages even before the war) and to a person who excels in a sport (from our use of "a crack right end," perhaps). Three supposedly English words we have so far been unable to track down are *motocrossman, tan sad,* and *surboum. Défi,* the literary term for "challenge," as to a duel, has been shifted to coincide with our own use of "challenge" in the educational sense. There are such spelling revisions in the Franglais borrowings as *ranche* and *sherif,* and French "phonetic" spellings like *Nouillorque* for New York and *iounite* for unite. Etiemble often distinguishes between British and American loans (*interval, site, vs. intermission, lot*).

But Etiemble does not stop at vocabulary. He considers the Atlantic Sabir a new language in its own right, and writes chapters dealing with its alphabet, spelling, pronunciation, punctuation, accentuation, morphology, syntax, and stylistics. This is obviously a spoof, but his examples are mostly drawn from the pages of contemporary French newspapers and magazines. The phrase *"Il est beaucoup parlé du fait que la France rajeunit,"* for instance, comes from *Le Midi libre; "La solution est loin d'être sous contrôle"* is from *Le Monde; "L'entière population française"* is from *Le Figaro.*

Etiemble's conclusions appear on the jacket of his book: "French, which until yesterday was still the universal tongue of the educated white man, is today, in the mouths of our fellow-citizens, nothing but a pidgin, ashamed of its illustrious past. Why do we speak Franglais? Everybody shares in the guilt: the press and women like Marie Chantal, the radio and the army, the government and the advertising industry, big politics and the basest interests. If ridicule could still kill, we might be able to cleanse ourselves of this scourge. But it will take far more. . . . So far as I am concerned, I refuse to say 'O.K.' to what is going on."

§   §   §

It is possible that Etiemble exaggerates. One can do a good deal if one deliberately sets out to seek the words and expressions that will suit his purpose. Nevertheless, the picture he paints is alarming, at least to those who believe in the purity of the French language.

They might take comfort from the fact that all languages have weathered similar storms, have managed to absorb and digest hundreds and thousands of importations, and have nevertheless survived. But when all is said and done, by the time the present cycle is completed, French will be closer to English, just as English was closer to French at the completion of the Norman Conquest. We, too, could be "waxing sore wroth" instead of merely "turning very enraged" at the *bouleversement* inflicted upon the English language by that historical event.

Shortly after the appearance of Etiemble's book, Spain's greatest language scholar, Ramón Menéndez-Pidal, issued a few measured and circumspect words of warning against the far too numerous penetrations of Spanish by English that are going on today. For German, our material is scanty, but Etiemble himself supplies such examples as a sign over a Frankfurt beauty parlor that reads: *Augen make up à la carte.* Three languages in six words constitute a very acceptable sample of the new European lingua franca.

Alfredo Tudisco, writing in the Milan *Corriere della Sera,* illustrates the English infiltration of the Italian language in this eloquent passage:

§   §   §

"È un vero playboy, molto sexy, il beniamino dell'international set; industrial design è il suo hobby, e di più è un health fiend; figurati, va dal dottore per un check-up ogni due mesi!"

§   §   §

But unlike Etiemble, Tudisco tells his Italian readers not to worry. English additions to the Italian language, he says, make the latter simpler and more up to date. "We can swallow our Anglicisms with our minds at ease," he concludes.

"The first favorable results are already apparent in the re-placement of complicated sentences full of subordinate clauses by simpler, clearer sentences based on co-ordinated structures." So it appears that somebody likes us after all.

The Japanese newspaper *Asahi* recently gave a long list of up-to-date borrowings from English. Recalling the general rule that Japanese replaces *l*'s with *r*'s, ends words in vowels or -*n*, and inserts vowels between any two or more consonant sounds, we should not find it hard to trace *disuku jokii* to disc jockey, *surogan* to slogan, *sumogu* to smog, *supiido* to speed, *misairu* to missile, *niyu sutairu* to new style, *gohe* to go ahead, *bakapu* to back up. Blends abound: *jazu kichigai* is jazz crazy. Then there are the puzzling transcriptions *kurosu wurudo pasaru* and *oo7-Sandaboru;* they stand for crossword puzzle and Thunderball. As in the case of Italian, there are no adverse comments from the compiler of the list.

There is little question that English is today making headway into the heart of assorted foreign territories, to a far greater degree than seemed possible at the close of World War II.

Will the trend continue? If it does, will the ultimate outcome be a world-wide International English? Or will it be a disjointed series of English pidgins? Will the great languages of the future be named *Franglais* (or Frenglish), *Espanglés* (or Spanglish), *Italinglese* (or Italenglish), *Deunglisch* (or Germanglish), even *Rusanglisky* and *Nihon-ei-go* (or Russenglish and Japanglish)?

PART FIVE

a b c d e f g h i j k l m n o p q r s t u v w x y z

A GLIMPSE INTO
THE FUTURE

WHAT WILL BE WILL BE, GRANTED. BUT IS THERE
any harm in looking into the omens?

There are two angles to the future of the English language. One is the possibility that it may march on to world use, in one form or another. The other is its own development on its own home soil.

Taking international aspects first, I shall begin by airing my own views as to the continuance of the trend outlined in the last section. There are also certain distorted (perhaps only over-simplified) points of view concerning the relationship between English spelling reform, English as an international language, and world peace, which I first endeavored to correct nearly twenty years ago, in an article that appeared in a professional journal (Chapter 21).

Next there are two chapters on the international aspects of present-day English, as reflected in its use in the so-called emerging nations, but in competition with its chief rival, French; and its use in the great mass communication media, films, radio, TV, Telstar. They round out the picture, but the reader is left to draw his own conclusions.

Lastly, I have included two chapters of prophecies about the future development of the English language on its own soil, shorn of all international considerations. The first is as cold, sober, and scientific as anything dealing with the future can be made. The second is merely good fun, and not meant to be taken too seriously. It represents the flight of one man's imagination as to what could conceivably happen to a language called upon to serve a twenty-first-century civilization. Others have tried their hand at this, ever since the days of H. G. Wells. The reader is advised to regard it as science fiction, not linguistic science.

CHAPTER TWENTY

A B C D E F G H I J K L M N O P Q R S T U V W X Y Z

The International Language and English

There is no question in my mind that by the end of the century a language for international use will be safely on its way, unless a world cataclysm, natural or man-made, intervenes. The modern world needs and demands such a language. Back in the nineteenth century, perhaps one person in a hundred had occasion at some time or other in the course of his lifetime to find himself in a country of different speech from his own. By the end of World War I, this ratio had shrunk to one in twenty-five. Today, it is roughly one in ten. By the year 2000, if present trends continue, it will be one in two. The travelers will by no means all be pleasure tourists, for whom linguistic accommodations are provided in exchange for hard currency. Even now, we have members of the Armed Forces, exchange students and teachers, civilian workers of all kinds, engineers and technicians, salesmen and business representatives, Peace Corpsmen, missionaries, diplomatic personnel. Other countries, like Spain, Greece, Italy, and Mexico, ship abroad vast numbers of migrant manual workers. Still others, like India, China, Puerto Rico, and Cuba, have millions of nationals living abroad on a more or less permanent basis, but retaining their own language and customs. As this flow continues and increases, the language traffic jam becomes a major headache. It will have to be solved, and the solution, when the time is ripe, will probably be on a crash basis, as is customary with all seemingly insoluble problems that must suddenly be solved.

A war in which one of the major participants were to emerge victorious might provide a ready-made solution. But the indications are that there will be no victors in the next war involving two or more first-class military powers. Solution by discussion, negotiation, and planning seems to be too much to hope for, at least in the immediate future. Major international bodies, such as UN and UNESCO, shun the international language problem as they would the plague. The men that constitute these bodies, and the governments they represent, find the linguistic *status quo* far more to their liking. For one thing, linguistic diversity lends itself to overheated nationalisms. The shibboleth of language, added to those of religious, political, and sociological ideology, outmoded customs and beliefs, territorial and economic ambitions, and the plain, unadulterated desire of politicians of all colors to run other people's lives for them, can be of signal help in pitting Arabs against Israelis, Indians against Pakistanis, Russians against Germans, Chinese against Americans.

All this may change in the not too remote future. The younger generations of numerous countries show by no uncertain signs that they do not wish to subscribe to the divisive shibboleths of the past. But if we are to deal with immediate realities, it may be well to concentrate our attention upon what is likely to happen, linguistically speaking, under conditions representing a continuation and extension of those that prevail today. With no atomic war and no intelligent discussion and choice guiding the course of the international language of the future, what is likely to emerge?

Constructed languages would probably represent intelligent choice, since one can put into a constructed language all the elements deemed desirable: complete regularity of grammatical scheme, complete standardization and phonetization, as much internationality and neutrality of vocabulary and structure as is practical. But a constructed language, without the backing of the world's governments, has little chance of success. Esperanto, by far the most successful and popular of all constructed languages, has—after eighty years of constant, indefatigable, even fanatical propaganda on the part of its enthusiasts—a body of speakers which even the rosiest estimates by the Esperantists themselves do not place beyond fifteen million out of a world population of three billion. At this rate of growth, and without the powerful intervention of the world powers that be, Esperanto would possibly make the grade around A.D. 10,000. But a world language will become a recognized must within the next thirty years.

Without war or intelligent official choice, what national language is likely to emerge as the one that will gradually be accepted and acquired by most of the world's people? What will happen to it when and if it is so accepted and acquired?

Again, let us look at the facts in the matter, as reported at the beginning of Part One. On a practical present-day basis, only a handful of national, official languages are in a position to be seriously considered as contenders—English, French, Spanish, Russian, Chinese.

Chinese, which has the largest speaking population, may be ruled out by reason of its poor world distribution, plus the fact that it has not yet achieved the commercial, economic, and technological development that a world language must have. Russian, which has both the population and the technical development, is short on distribution and the commercial-economic factor. Spanish has a highly lopsided distribution and insufficient commercial-economic-technical development, in addition to lacking the political-military factor of a first-rate power. French, with distribution, commercial-economic and technical development, is short on population. English, with the second largest body of native speakers on earth, first-class distribution, economic, com-mercial, technical development of the highest order, and first-class political-military power, seems the logical candidate.

This picture is clearly brought out by international reactions. In all non-English-speaking countries where a direct poll was taken as to popular preference in the matter of an international language, English easily came out the winner, with at least sixty per cent of the votes. (Such a poll was taken in 1950 by the Gallup Institute in Norway, Hol-land, and Finland, and in 1961 by a Japanese organization in Japan.) What would happen if the poll were made world-wide, and communist countries included, is anybody's guess. But the language that is directly accessible to one out of ten people throughout the world, and indirectly accessible to one out of three; that is most widely studied internationally; that combines the outer limits of economic, commercial, technological, political, and military power, does seem to impress most people as the language destined for world use, if extraneous factors do not intervene.

This is sensed by all advocates of English, including people in official capacities, and is probably the main un-spoken reason why they do not at all respond to pleas for a solution based on an intelligent, deliberate choice. Why upset the applecart? Why interfere with a situation that offers such favorable omens, at least on the surface? This means that the American and British governments find it expedient to be perennially evasive about the question of a world language, even while they unofficially (but not un-obtrusively) push English with all the means in their power, including USIA libraries, British Institute schools, Ford Foundation grants, and even foreign missions (the Rev. Frank Laubach has flatly declared that on the basis of his observations in the course of his extensive travels in under-developed regions, English is going to be the international language).

The opposition comes mainly from speakers of French, who lose no opportunity to remind everyone of the international role of French in the past, and are sometimes quite vociferous about it (Etiemble, for example, reminds us that in many countries French is still a compulsory subject in the secondary schools, while English is not; in Italy, to my own knowledge, the number of students of French in all grades is still five times that of students of English); from the Esperantists, who will insist to their dying gasp upon an intelligent, negotiated solution; and from the communist countries, which regard the English language as the vehicle of Anglo-American imperialism, colonialism, capitalism, and all the other alleged evils they deplore. But the communist countries find it expedient to use English in their international subversion plots, and their opposition, which was at one time extremely vocal, has of late become muted. The reason for this, in my opinion, is not that they have changed their minds and hearts, but rather that with two big forms of national communism in competition, they find it difficult to push either Russian or Chinese; and that since their master plan involves world subversion to communism, they figure that once they are politically in the saddle they can impose their languages, or even adapt international English to their own purposes, changing its content and function from that of mouthpiece of capitalism to that of the Voice of Communism. This, by the way, is something that past linguistic history shows us can rather easily be done, by a deliberate process of indoctrination and wholesale semantic change: witness how Latin, the Voice of Roman Imperialism, turned into the mouthpiece of the universal Christian Church.

§ § §

So much for the facts. Other considerations may be subjective and of slight relevance in the factual picture, but since most people insist on viewing things subjectively, they inevitably tend to inject themselves into any discussion on the subject.

To begin with, there is little question that English is,

as it was painted by earlier communist writers and is still painted in the writings of many citizens of non-communist lands (Etiemble, for instance), the carrier of Anglo-American cultural imperialism, neo-colonialism (of the kind typified in our overseas adventures), and, above all, not so much capitalism as commercialism.

Cultural imperialism is what it is, and not much can be done about it. It stands to reason that a leader of an under-developed country trained and educated in the United States, Britain, or France, as so many of them are, will absorb the culture of the land that educated him, and that this culture will color his thinking even while he rants against the colonialist power that trained him.

Neo-colonialism is also something for which there is little remedy. If the backward nations want to be helped out of their backwardness, they must to some extent submit to the leadership of the nations that have the know-how. It may be remarked in passing that the Russians and Chinese are at least as guilty of neo-colonialistic practices as are the Americans, British, or French.

Commercialism may be deplorable, at least in its more extreme manifestations, but it is precisely the sort of thing other nations want, because by and large it leads to a higher standard of living and material prosperity that appeals to at least nine out of every ten people, no matter in what country they live.

There is little point in English speakers, American or British, apologizing for these three things. Shorn of the semantic charges that have been attached to these words, they represent progress—the type of progress every nation, including the communist ones, is trying to achieve. We, the speakers of English, should proudly flaunt the banners of cultural imperialism, neo-colonialism, and commercialism. The first places us in the forefront of intellectual and edu-cational progress; the second proves that we are scientifically and technologically in the lead; the third points the way to a better material life for everybody concerned.

A second category of subjective criticism of the English language is concerned with the difficulties of its sound structure, grammatical constructions, and idiomatic word groups. These are real enough, but they affect only foreign learners of the language, who approach it at the adult stage, when language habits are firmly set. They do not affect native speakers, who learn the language from childhood by the natural speaking process. If English were to become a true international language, all, or practically all, would learn it that way. At any rate, from the point of view of the adult learner, all foreign languages are fraught with infinite difficulties. Adult foreign learners of English actually seem to do better than adult English-speaking learners of other tongues.

One final consideration gives us pause. If English were to spread to the point of becoming a common language for the whole world, would we run the risk of seeing it fragment itself into an infinite number of pidgins such as we saw in Chapter 4? Already writers in India are deploring the fact that the Indian schools are no longer producing speakers of the sort of polished English that flourished in the past, while African writers complain about the "barbarism" of Nigerian and Tanzanian English. There is the danger, some say, that if English (or any other tongue selected for world use) ever spreads far enough, it will give rise to new dialects that will eventually become separate and mutually incomprehensible languages. Here the reader may be referred to my description of the role of present-day means of communication (TV, radio, films) in Chapter 23. Under such conditions, languages tend to become standardized and uniform, not to break down into separate dialects as they once did and kept on doing to the dawn of our century.

The omens for World English, at the present moment and in relation to present trends, are favorable. Whether they will remain so is another matter. History is full of imponderables, strange surprises, and unexpected reversals.

CHAPTER TWENTY-ONE

ABCDEFGHIJKLMNOPQRSTUVWXYZ

One World? One Language?[1]

We have lately been deluged, from the offices of *Modern Language Journal* and other sources, with books, booklets, pamphlets, and leaflets the aim of which is to advocate the reform of English spelling so as to bring it in line with pronunciation.

In itself, this is a praiseworthy objective. The difficulties which strew its path are neither few nor inconsiderable. They have been summarized in an earlier chapter.

But there is a curious undertone that runs through the majority of present-day writings on the subject, a series of logical or illogical assumptions and syllogisms. English, purged of its traditional spelling and phonetically written, will, it is claimed, at once become the international language; once an international language is achieved, wars will cease. By reforming English spelling, we can secure its international adoption, and thereby prevent future wars.

Were all this true, it might be well worth while making the effort. Perhaps we should make it anyway, for our own satisfaction and to save our schoolchildren from the tiresome task of learning to spell. But ought we not first to consult the other nations and find out whether they would be willing to accept a simplified-spelling English as a tongue of

[1] The point of view that this brief article criticizes, while perhaps not quite so prevalent today, is still widespread.

common intercourse? If they say Yes, we might try leaving the other problem, that of war, to take care of itself. But what if they say No?

Some of the proponents of spelling reform do not seem to think that any foreign country will be able to withstand the obvious attractions of the English language once it is phoneticized. One writer appears to have some conception of the difficulties of the problems of acceptance when he writes: "We could yield a lot to Russia in exchange for their cooperation. Someone must yield on this point, and it is generally agreed by scholars and statesmen that English is the most suitable for general use." Berlin to East Germany, a communist government in South Vietnam, and recognition of Red China in exchange for International English?

Elsewhere in my writings, I proposed what seemed then, and still seems now, a more logical procedure, if a consensus solution is what we want. Let the governments, if they are really interested in the creation of a world language to facilitate international communication, appoint a commission of competent linguists with all nations represented in proportion to their literate populations. Let this commission proceed like our own nominating conventions, with all members free to nominate the language of their choice, national or constructed. Then let a series of run-off elections be held, with half the languages nominated dropping out at each voting, until an absolute majority is reached for one tongue. If the final decision is won by a national language, let that language be completely phoneticized and standardized for international use (constructed languages, like Esperanto or Interlingua, are already fully phoneticized and standardized). Let it be put into all the elementary schools in the world on a footing of perfect equality with the local language, to be learned by the natural, spoken method, not by the grammar-translation method so often deprecated in our high-school teaching of foreign languages. The new generations of all lands will then grow up completely bilingual, equipped with their own national and also with the international tongue.

The older generations would be perfectly free to learn the new international language or not to learn it. If they did, it would be at the adult stage, by the painful process. But it would be no worse than learning any foreign tongue; in fact, it would be easier, in view of the complete phoneticization of the international tongue. Should the choice fall on English, we would have two brands of English, coinciding in speech (up to a point) but differing in writing: American-British English, with its antiquated spelling, and International English, with phonetic spelling. Once International English had the assurance of world-wide acceptance, few Americans or Englishmen would refuse to learn it in its new, simplified written form.

But the choice of the linguistic congress might fall on another tongue—French, Spanish, Russian, Interglossa, or Novial. If so, it would be up to the advocates of spelling reform to abide by the decision of the majority, to leave traditional English spelling alone, unless they would still want to reform it for purely internal consumption, and proceed to learn, or at least let the younger English-speaking generations learn, International French, or International Russian, or Esperanto, or Latino Sine Flexione.

What would happen to the national languages? Advocates of international tongues (Basic English, Esperanto, and the like) are forever assuring us that the tongue they favor would be used *only* for international purposes, that it would not displace the existing languages within their national borders. I do not share this view. In the long run, languages of lesser currency would be made obsolete by a language of universal currency, but the process would take centuries. Present-day teachers and students of foreign languages would continue to flourish at least as long as they. Even after the two or three centuries it would take to make them obsolete, English, French, Spanish, Italian, and German would still be studied exclusively for their cultural value, as Latin and Greek are studied at present.

What of the danger of dialectalization of the new international tongue, of its splitting up into numerous local languages, as Latin did after the fall of the Roman Empire? It would take another "fall of the Roman Empire" to do it, with complete disruption of present-day communications and international interchanges. While we have the railroad, the steamship, the automobile, the plane, the radio, TV, and films, the international language would not dialectalize. It would become more and more unified.

What of the question of war? Will an international language bring about the end of mankind's greatest scourge? Not unless it is accompanied by a will to end war and by an effective international organization that will make war impossible. History is far too full of examples of wars between nations, cities, and groups speaking the same language. Full linguistic understanding is a powerful aid to peace, but it must be complemented by something much more difficult to achieve—the will for peace, and a truly efficient peace machinery.

There is no doubt, however, that if future wars must come in spite of an international language, the latter will tend to make them far less uncomfortable for all their participants. It will also eliminate such unnecessary deaths as that of the American general (if the press account is true) who was shot because he did not understand what his German captors were saying to him and thought, erroneously, that they wanted him to hand over his pistol, for which he reached.

By all means let us strive for (a) the reform of English spelling; (b) the achievement of an international language; (c) the end of wars. But let us keep the three issues and their implications separate in our minds and discussions, and not scramble them together in the fashion of a Spanish omelet.

The Hidden Politics
of Words[1]

Political institutions change faster than linguistic practices. It is therefore not surprising that the linguistic fruits of colonialism live on, and that they seem destined to live on for decades and perhaps even centuries after colonialism itself has become largely a thing of the past. What is surprising is how often these fruits are overlooked or, in some cases, magnified beyond all reason. Here, once again, is powerful proof that the word, both written and spoken, is by no means the passive, powerless thing many people unthinkingly assume it is.

Colonialism is an ancient phenomenon, and its linguistic repercussions can be studied at leisure in history books. The Romans, for example, extended not only their sway but also their language and culture to hundreds of alien groups, ultimately building up an empire that stretched from the

---

1 This article originally bore the subtitle: "Colonialism may be a dying phase in international affairs, but the colonialism of language still flourishes—with some bizarre and unexpected effects."

English and French, the two great colonial languages, continue to expand in areas from which the political dominance of their speakers has been largely excluded. This is a present-day phenomenon with which we must reckon. Its implications for what concerns the future of the English language are obvious.

North German forests to the edge of the Sahara, from the Atlantic to the Persian Gulf. In a large portion of this immense area their language endured long after their empire had crumbled, and the Romance tongues of Portugal, Spain, France, Italy, and Rumania, not to mention those of more than half the Western Hemisphere, are there today to attest to the enduring qualities of linguistic colonialism.

Or, in more recent times, consider the case of Ireland. Originally a Celtic-speaking land that was invaded but not really occupied by England's Norman barons and their Saxon retainers as far back as the twelfth century, and subsequently brought under English rule in the days of Elizabeth and Cromwell, Ireland held on as stubbornly to her Celtic language as to her Catholic faith. It is estimated that just before the great potato famine of the late 1840's, when her population had reached a high-water mark of about 8,000,000, well over half the Irish still spoke Gaelic. By 1851, only 1,500,-000 Gaelic speakers remained out of the 4,000,000 who had not died or migrated to America. By the beginning of this century, only about 650,000 Gaelic speakers were left in Ireland, approximately fifteen per cent of the total population. The rest of the Irish had simply forgotten their Gaelic. They spoke only English, with or without a brogue. Even today, in spite of the strenuous efforts of the Irish government to bring back Gaelic, barely twenty per cent of the population speaks it. But with the exception of a few thousand diehards in the Gaeltacht (the southwestern region where Gaelic always continued to be spoken), all Irishmen speak English, the tongue of colonization. This is not because of love for England or her language. It is simply a matter of convenience, coupled with an unspoken recognition of the fact that a language spoken in every corner of the earth, and in which you can directly communicate with more than one tenth of the world's population, is better for practical purposes than a tongue, however ancient and beautiful, that serves you only within the confines of the Emerald Isle, and none too widely even there.

The new countries that have sprouted up like mushrooms all over the map may be quite vocal in UN circles and in their own press when they deplore both old and new colonialism. But they tend to live on with it, consciously or unconsciously, in many aspects of their economies, international policies, and world outlook. For this there are, of course, excellent reasons. Former French or British colonies whose economy was closely linked to that of France or Britain, whose systems of education, banking, military service, taxation, transportation, and all the other things that the twentieth-century world is made up of, were created and conducted by the French or British, cannot be expected to sever all their links overnight, under penalty of sinking back into chaos. What is surprising is that few of them show any tendency even to consider the possibility of loosening those links, now or in the future. If anything, the links tend to be drawn tighter.

Nowhere is this more apparent than in language. As the European colonizers of the sixteenth to the nineteenth centuries took possession of alien lands in the exploitable continents, sometimes by peaceful means, more often simply by force of superior armaments, they brought their languages with them and imposed them on the colonial populations as official tongues of common intercourse. Whatever we may think of the method, this generally turned out to be a blessing to the native populations, since it gave them a common means of communication where, because of the vast number and diversity of local languages and dialects, none had existed before. In Nigeria, for example, speakers of Ewe, Efik, Fanti, and Hausa were finally able to talk to one another in the English of their conquerors. The same may be said even for a land of ancient and noble civilization like India, where the speakers of Tamil and Telugu of the south discovered that they could communicate in English with the speakers of Hindi, Bengali, Gujarati, and Punjabi of the north, without having in any way to defer to the language or culture of their fellow Indians of different ethnic affiliations.

This possibility of intercommunication by using the language of the colonizing power extended, however, only to that intellectual élite, often a very small portion of the total population, that had the good fortune to be educated in the schools set up by the colonizers, and possibly even to be sent to the "stepmother" country to complete their education. But it would be unwise to minimize the role played by this intellectual élite, not only in the general life of the country, but in taking the lead in movements designed to end the colonial status of their lands and set them up as full-fledged independent nations. Such men as Nehru and Kenyatta were the products of British schools. Tshombe and Lumumba were educated in Belgium, Ho Chi Minh and Bourguiba in France, Sukarno in Holland. However much these leaders may abhor colonialism as an institution, it is to their respective colonizing powers that they owe both their cultural formation and their positions of leadership.

It may be only a small fraction of the population of countries like Malawi and Zambia that speak English, or of Gabon and Guinea that speak French. But this small fraction effectively rules the country and directs its activities. Its outlook is, in a sense, British or French. Even when the leaders meet, as they did at Bandung, to deplore colonialism, they are forced to use the language of a colonizing power in order to understand each other.

In a few of the former colonial countries, attempts are being made to break the linguistic chains that bind the countries to their former colonial masters. Perhaps the most successful of these attempts are Indonesia's creation of a new national tongue to supersede both the Dutch of the colonizers and the myriad tongues of the Indonesian islands, and the setting up by the Republic of the Philippines of one of the more widespread local languages, Tagalog, as a national tongue to replace both the recent English of the Americans and the old veneer left by the Spaniards. In Indonesia, the career of Bahasa Indonesia, the newly created national tongue, has been mightily aided by the fact that Bahasa is based squarely upon an older lingua franca, Malay (the Dutch called it Bazaar Malay), that already served as a language of common intercourse among the speakers of the hundred tongues of the thousand islands that were once the Netherlands East Indies. In spite of this, and in spite of the rather strenuous educational and anti-illiteracy efforts exerted by Sukarno's government, it is estimated that barely twenty million out of Indonesia's hundred million people are today able to use Bahasa acceptably.

In the Philippines, by latest accounts, Tagalog seems to be making slow progress. It is the mother tongue of only about a fifth of the Republic's population of 30,000,000 or more; it is outstripped by Visayan in the number of speakers, has Ilocano and Bikol as runners-up, and must overcome the resistance of the two languages of colonization, Spanish and English, both of which are spoken, read, and written by most literate Filipinos.

One country where the campaign to get rid of the language of colonization came spectacularly a cropper is India. Here it had been the intention of Nehru's government to get rid, once and for all, of English, which is spoken, in one fashion or another, by perhaps 25,000,000 out of the country's estimated population of about 480,000,000. The replacement was to be Hindi, an Indo-Aryan language of the north that is the mother tongue of perhaps 160,000,000 (its variant, Urdu, is official in neighboring Pakistan, where it is spoken by perhaps a fifth of a total population of 100,000,000). The plan had originally been to eliminate English and use Hindi as the sole national tongue by 1965, but with thirteen other regional languages, all on a basis of parity with Hindi within their own speaking areas. As the date approached, there was such a storm of protest from the Dravidian-speaking states of the south that Premier Shastri was forced to suspend execution of the plan, assuring the dissident states that English would continue to remain in force as a co-official language as long as the south should desire it. This reassurance, however, came only after nearly one hundred people had lost their lives in the Madras language riots. As matters now stand, each Indian state has three official languages: English, Hindi, and the predominant local tongue. More English is being studied in India than ever before, though some Indians shake their heads and assert that modern educational systems will never produce English speakers of the caliber of Nehru and Mme Pandit.

Pakistan retained English as a co-official language with Urdu at the time of the partition of British India, and has never made any serious effort to displace it, even when the Bengali speakers of East Pakistan forced recognition of their language on a co-official basis in their area. Ceylon, which replaced English with Sinhalese in 1957, now wishes it had retained it, in view of the frequent rioting of the Tamil-speaking part of the population. Burma, another nation that acquired its independence from Britain after World War II, still has English on a co-official basis with Burmese. Two of the four nations into which French Indochina was ultimately carved (South Vietnam and Laos) continue to use French on a co-official basis with Vietnamese and Laotian, respectively. Cambodia and North Vietnam do not, but French continues in widespread use in both countries.

It is on the African continent, however, that the triumph of the former tongues of colonization is almost complete, with replacement seldom if ever thought of. French alone is official in Chad, Dahomey, Gabon, Guinea, Ivory Coast, Mali, Senegal, Togo, and Upper Volta, in addition to being co-official in Algeria, the Central African Republic, Burundi, Rwanda, the Malagasy Republic, and the Brazzaville Congo. In the Leopoldville Congo (the former Belgian Congo), only the two colonizing languages, French and Flemish, are official. English alone holds sway in Gambia, Kenya, Liberia, Uganda, and Zambia. It is co-official in Tanzania (including the former Zanzibar), Niger, Nigeria, Sierra Leone, and Ghana. In Malawi, the two fully official languages are both colonial: English and Afrikaans. In Somalia, English is co-official with Italian and Arabic, both of which may be described as former tongues of colonization. There is, in addition, semi-official status for French in Morocco, Tunisia, the United Arab Republic (Egypt), Niger, Mauritania, even Ghana; and for English in the United Arab Republic and the Sudan.

Few African languages, apart from the two Semitic tongues that originally came from Arabia (Arabic and Amharic), have made the grade to full officiality. Amharic is the sole official tongue of Ethiopia (though French, English, and Italian are rather widely spoken), while Arabic appears not only in the Arab states of North Africa (Morocco, Algeria, Tunisia, Libya, the United Arab Republic, the Sudan), but also in Somalia, Niger, and Eritrea. The one and only Malayo-Polynesian tongue of Africa, Malagasy, is co-official with French in the former Madagascar. Languages that may be described as fully African Negro, and that are used on a co-official basis with the tongues of colonization, are the Sangho of the Central African Republic, the Kirundi of Burundi, the Mouman and Kutuba of the Brazzaville Congo, the Hausa of Nigeria and Niger, the Swahili of Tanzania, the Kinyarwanda of Rwanda, the Krio of Sierra Leone, and the Twi, Fanti, Ga, and Ewe of Ghana. But these languages, with the exception of Swahili and Hausa, are purely local, undeveloped, and serve only a fraction of the population even in the countries where they are official. Everywhere in the new African countries there is a thirst for education and literacy—in English, or French, or both.

Highly instructive to me was an experience I had four years ago while serving as Mellon Visiting Professor at the University of Pittsburgh. The university was host to a visiting delegation of some twenty black Africans of standing—educators, bankers, scientists, industrialists. They were touring the United States to observe firsthand our Western civilization and report back to their respective countries. All of them came from nations that had been carved out of the former French and Belgian African empires. None of them could speak any English. All spoke fluent, almost flawless French. They had with them an interpreter for their American contacts. Among themselves, they used nothing but French. Not one of them knew the African language of any other. They supplied the key to the African picture, at least south of the Sahara. The great colonial languages, French and English, offer the Africans not only access to the outside world, but even ready-made means of intercommunication. In the Nigerian election campaign, in scenes that were flashed on American TV screens the candidates were heard to use English in their campaign speeches, and the announcer explained that if they had tried to use any of the local languages, they would have reached only a fraction of their audiences. As it was, there were always enough English speakers in the crowd to relay the candidate's message to the others, in all the different tongues and dialects of the region.

Among the African Negro languages there are at least two, Hausa and Swahili, that could conceivably be expanded for general use in the same fashion that Nehru tried to expand Hindi and Sukarno tried to expand Bahasa. Both have at least 10,000,000 speakers, not to mention fairly extensive speaking areas, and are also tongues of great beauty and flexibility, with vocabularies that can be enlarged at will to betoken modern concepts. What seems to be missing is the desire to use them. The press of the African countries continues to be overwhelmingly French and English, with only an occasional attempt at using a native tongue.

Again, it must be emphasized that while the general African attitude is not such as to give comfort to Negro cultural nationalists, it is intensely practical and utilitarian. Countries that are striving to bring themselves into line with twentieth-century civilization feel forced to make use of the tools of that civilization, including language. A speaker of Kinyarwanda sees no reason to acquire a tongue of limited range, even a fairly widespread one like Swahili, when

French and English are there to give him access to the whole wide world.

So linguistic colonialism continues to flourish and expand, even while its political counterpart is dying out. Perhaps the phenomenon we observe in the former colonial lands, particularly in Africa, is only a reflection of a larger linguistic picture, one that tends inevitably toward a single tongue for world-wide use, one in which all men, swallowing their national pride, will be able to communicate directly and practically, in an age when transportation has become easy and rapid and international travel is a commonplace instead of a rare experience reserved for the chosen few.

It may also be pointed out that the fruits of linguistic and even cultural colonialism in the past have been far from bad. The Romanization of customs and citizenship, and the Latinization of speech, of ancient populations with such diverse backgrounds as the Gauls, Iberians, Oscans, Etruscans, Numidians, and Dacians cannot, in the light of history, be described as having done those populations any irreparable damage; quite the contrary, to judge from the exploits of their descendants.

What TV Is Doing
to Language

Television is by far the most powerful agent of linguistic
change the world has ever known. In this function it has
already, in the few years of its existence, outstripped both
literacy and universal compulsory education.

This may seem a gross exaggeration. Yet consider: both
literacy and universal compulsory education bear primarily
upon the written language, which even in these days of
widespread reading and writing accounts for less than ten
per cent of our total communication. Television bears primarily upon the spoken tongue, which is communication's
primary tool, to the extent that almost ninety per cent of
all communication uses it as a medium. One may quibble
about the relative importance of the content of written as
against spoken communication. One may even reasonably
advance the claim that the sort of communication that really
counts, and is therefore embodied into permanent records,
is primarily written; that "words fly away, but written mes-
sages endure," as the Latin saying put it two thousand years
ago; that there is no basic significance to at least fifty per
cent of the oral interchange that goes on among all sorts of
persons, high and low. But there are equally cogent counter-
arguments. Today, permanent records may be inscribed on
discs and tapes, to be stored away and repeated at will, and
even combined, TV-style, with a lifelike picture. This means

that words no longer "fly away." In fact, they may be blended with the image of their speaker, to endure as a perennial record both of the speaker and of what he said.

But this is only a side issue, like that other recent discovery of the outside world (the professional linguists had known it for decades) that each individual's recorded voice, traced visually on a spectrogram, is as distinctive as are his fingerprints, and constitutes just as sure a means of positive identification. The point that concerns us is that at no time in history prior to the present has there been so powerful and swift-working an instrument of linguistic change as the one supplied today by TV, flanked by two other recent innovations that share some of its characteristics, radio and film.

The younger generations of all countries, exposed to a steady, inexorable bombardment of the standard national language dispensed by movie actors, radio announcers, and, above all, TV newscasters, anchormen, advertisers, and feature actors, are well on the way to discarding all the dialectal features of their parents' speech and adopting the standard tongue they hear on their favorite programs, spoken by people who have in their eyes the highest prestige.

Let me illustrate. Italy is a land of numerous and persistent dialects. Even where the Italian speaker is thoroughly educated and speaks with full command of both grammar and vocabulary, it seldom fails that his local intonation shines through and acts as a dead giveaway of his regional background. I left my native Italy in 1908, at the age of seven; returning for the first time in 1921, at the age of twenty, and landing in Genoa, I was a bit surprised to be told by a Genoese student: "You're a Roman, aren't you?" My native intonation had given me away.

But that was in pre-TV days. In 1959, riding a Naples bus with a Neapolitan friend, I was surprised to hear a group of young people on the bus speaking a correct, unidentifiable general Italian from which all features of local intonation were absent. I asked my friend whether they could be tourists from central Italy. "Not at all," he replied, "they are local boys and girls." "But what about the Neopolitan accent, which no Neapolitan has ever been known to lose, no matter how educated?" "Is that so?" came the answer. "Wait until we get home and you'll find out." When we arrived at my friend's apartment, I made the acquaintance of his three children, aged eight, ten, and twelve. All spoke in the same unidentifiable general Italian I had heard on the bus, though Papa and Mamma kept on speaking, as they had always done, in their own cultured Neapolitan. "This" said my friend, "is what is happening all over Italy. The youngsters don't take their language from their parents and relatives any more. In part, they take it from the schools. But we had schools, too, in our days. What really makes the difference is films, radio, and, above all, TV. Those are the speakers who carry prestige in their eyes, and whom they consciously or unconsciously imitate. If this sort of thing goes on for another fifty years, there won't be a trace of a dialect left in Italy. All Italians will be speaking the same flat, monotonous, colorless national language. Maybe it's a blessing, maybe a curse. There won't be so much local color, but everybody will be able to understand everybody else, which is more than could be said of our generation."

Even before this revelation, I had been conscious of the same phenomenon in the English-speaking world. I had noticed how, with the first spoken British films, much of what was said was unintelligible to the American ear. Then we got used to the British accent, as they undoubtedly got used to ours. Now we take David Niven, *Secret Agent, The Avengers* in our stride, and think absolutely nothing of it. But don't imagine for a minute that it is all pure passive acceptance. There is also an insensible active merging of the two pronunciations. Our speech becomes more British, as the British speech becomes more American. If one day, a century or so from now, the two mainstreams of the English language, which began to diverge with the founding of the Jamestown and Plymouth Bay colonies, converge again into a single mighty river, to film, radio, and especially TV will go the power and the glory.

What happens internationally happens also locally. If you want to hear the general American of the future, Hollywood and TV-studio based, go to California and listen to the speech of the California-born younger generation (not, of course, to the immigrants from other states, who will carry their local intonations with them to their dying day). Do you recall how in the Presidential campaign of 1960 Kennedy's *ahsk* and *Africar* stood out like sore thumbs, while Nixon never drew a lifted eyebrow? Nixon spoke the general American of the future, an American shorn of all local peculiarities. A couple of years ago, Miss Arkansas became Miss America. Brought up on a diet of films, radio, TV, and one or two eastern colleges, she addressed the TV audience in a general American that bore absolutely no trace of Southern influence. Then Papa and Mamma were asked to say a few words. Arkansas honey simply dripped from their lips as they spoke. One thing is certain. Miss Arkansas's future children, brought up under modern conditions, will be using their mother's general American, not their grandparents' Southern intonation.

The omens are clear enough for what concerns individual national tongues. They are being and will be standardized and unified by our modern communications media. Whether all traces of local dialects will finally be obliterated it is difficult to prophesy, but certainly they will be driven more and more into the background. The time will come when it will require a real expedition into the Appalachian fastnesses to get a recording of the Ozarks speech, and when the last surviving speakers of Brooklynese will be hunted down by the linguists for recording purposes in the wilds of Greenpoint and Flatbush as were the last speakers of the dialect of Veglia in the Adriatic at the end of the last century.

§   §   §

But there is another entrancing facet to the situation. With the spreading of films, short-wave broadcasts, and Telstar programs all over the earth, what is going to happen to the language of *international* communication? Will there be a generalization of the dubbing and translating processes now in use, or will audiences grow impatient of the translated medium and demand and adapt themselves to some form of international language that will have world-wide currency?

No less a communications expert than General David Sarnoff of RCA makes a prophecy. It is his view, if he has been correctly quoted, that international communication, particularly for TV purposes, will evolve a type of common language that will be universally understood by all viewers, in whatever country they may be and whatever may be their national tongue.

For what my opinion may be worth, I find myself in agreement with David Sarnoff. There is no question in my mind that by the end of the century international communication of all kinds will have reached a point where a language for world-wide use will be an absolute necessity, not a topic for academic discussion. Gallup and similar polls taken both in the United States and abroad indicate that fully eighty-five per cent of all people polled anticipate such a development, and that they would look with favor upon a world language to be introduced in all the school systems of the world, on the kindergarten and elementary level, side by side with the national languages, to be imparted by natural speech methods (not taught as a high school or college subject) to all the new generations, so that all may grow up bilingual.

David Sarnoff, again if correctly quoted, anticipates that the new language of radio and TV communication will be largely based on English. A certain amount of doubt attaches to this part of his prophecy, particularly if the nature of the international language is to be officially determined by an international body, such as UN or UNESCO. English as a world-wide international language may under those circumstances run into heavy opposition, based partly on cultural rivalry (such opposition might well be expected from French speakers, who think their language should have the honor), partly on ideological factors (communist nations may well accuse the English language of being the voice of capitalism, imperialism, and neo-colonialism). If an official choice does not take place, and events are left free to run their course, it is more likely that David Sarnoff's prophecy will come true.

English-speaking countries control well over half the spoken communication media (movies, radio, TV) in the world. This means that they spill over their own borders and offer their programs, in their language, to the nations of continental Europe, Asia, Africa, Latin America, even Australasia. There is a reverse flow, to be sure. But here we come across another characteristic phenomenon. When communist countries like the U.S.S.R and China beam their propaganda broadcasts to the underdeveloped lands, they do it, as often as not, in English, because English is the best way of reaching the largest number of people who have access to the communication media. Kenya, Somalia, Thailand, India, Pakistan get a good deal of their communist indoctrination in our language; the recipients who own a radio or TV set, or who are able to attend a movie performance, translate willingly to the rest.

English is the language most widely studied in the secondary school systems of practically all countries, including the communist ones, particularly Russia and China, where well over half of all high school and college students take up, in a very serious way, the study of English. This is not because they love us. But they realize that so long as the English-speaking countries are in the forefront of mechanical and scientific progress, it behooves them to learn from us. The countries that neither love nor hate us nevertheless admire us for our material progress. They desire to attain not necessarily our ideology, but certainly our standard of living. Our customs and ways, many of them open to serious criticism, get around. So do the words and expressions that denote them. It is no accident that Etiemble in France thunders out against the infiltration of the French language by such English words and expressions as *week-end, sexy, pin-up, gangster, best seller,* etc. *Franglais,* he claims, is the weird combination of French and English which American commercialism has foisted on France. But the same "commercialism" has foisted approximately the same number of loan words, reprehensible and otherwise, on Spanish, Italian, German, Japanese, even to some extent Russian. Under the circumstances, and with the mighty aid of mass communication, it will not be at all surprising if Sarnoff's prophecy comes true in due course. What we shall then have will be an international language or pidgin, based largely upon English, but with suitable contributions from other important tongues, that will serve, in fairly efficient fashion, the international communications needs of the twenty-first century.

§   §   §

Meanwhile, let us not overlook the basic salutary effect that these media have had so far in revising the linguistic thinking and international outlook of English speakers. At the outset, the communication industries were as isolationist as the rest of us. Motion pictures were set in foreign locales with little attention to linguistic realism, and people of obviously different language backgrounds were portrayed as communicating easily and fluently in an English that logically they could not speak. Today, TV series like *Combat* and *I Spy* observe all the canons of reality. German troops and Chinese agents use German and Chinese among themselves, and the English-speaking audiences are left to figure out what they said either from the action or from a conveniently placed translator who is one of the characters. Even TV and radio commercials have gone in for linguistic realism in a big way: *"Nous les fumeurs de Tareyton préférons nous battre plutôt que changer de marque!"*; *"Pero no te limpiaste los dientes con Gleam. ¡Ay, qué niña!"* A certain brand of beer is advertised by characters dancing their native dances and singing lilting drinking songs in their own languages, and before the announcer tells you that we must be doing something right, he reminds you that in New York there are more Hungarian speakers than in Mohács and Debrecen combined, and he pronounces the place names in impeccable Magyar.

Of course all this is done to sell products. But the by-product is the arousing of an international consciousness in the American viewer, who is given the knowledge that other languages exist and are spoken, some idea of what they sound like, and the realization that their speakers have human reactions that do not differ too much from his own.

As a linguist interested in spreading knowledge and information about foreign languages among English speakers, as an advocate of linguistic standardization within each language for purposes of rapid and easy communication, and as a believer in the ultimate emergence of an international language for world-wide use, I cannot help viewing recent developments in the great modern communications media—of which TV is the most universally practical and satisfactory—with undiluted approval. TV may originally have been devised as primarily an instrument of commercialism, and only secondarily of public information and education. As time goes on, and with the full knowledge of its sponsors, TV, like film and radio before it, is turning into the most powerful tool the world has ever known for international education, linguistic unification, both on the national and international level, and (why not admit it?) international understanding, with all the attendant implications for human welfare and prosperity, peace, and the removal of the nightmare of atomic war that has been haunting our dreams since Hiroshima.

CHAPTER TWENTY-FOUR

ABCDEFGHIJKLMNOPQRSTUVWXYZ

English in 2067: A Forecast

If a modern Rip Van Winkle went to sleep and didn't wake up for a hundred years, how well would he understand an American of 2067?

Educated laymen know that the language they speak was once Elizabethan English (a little difficult to follow today, especially in the pronunciation of Shakespearean actors), and before that the half-incomprehensible language of Chaucer, and before that the Anglo-Saxon that few today can read, let alone speak, unless they have taken a graduate course in it. Yet many people fail to realize that language is also going to change in the future. The English of one thousand years from now (granted that English is still a living tongue by A.D. 2067) will probably be as different from the language of *Saturday Review* as the latter is from the tongue of *Beowulf*.

The big difference between the past and the future is that we know, or can reconstruct with some degree of accuracy, what has happened in the past, while we have no way of knowing—or so it sometimes seems—what course the future will take.

But is the last proposition altogether true? We know that governments, business organizations, even private individuals make projections into the future, based on present tendencies and trends. These forecasts do not, of course, have the same value as recorded history, since they may be thrown completely out of kilter by the unexpected or accidental, which is something that history takes in its stride, recording it after it happens. Nevertheless, barring the unexpected, it is quite possible for our government experts to say: "We anticipate that the population of the United States, growing at an average yearly rate of about two million, will reach the 200 million mark, more or less, by 1970." In like manner, a business firm may say: "Our profits have grown about $1 million a year over the past ten years. Barring a major depression, we estimate that by 1970 they will be about $3 million higher than they are today." When you estimate your income tax for a year that is just beginning, as the Treasury Department somewhat unreasonably asks you to do, you go through this process of reasoning: "My income over the past five years has been about $10,000. As of this moment, I cannot anticipate any sizable change. Therefore, I am putting down the same figures for 1967 that appear in my 1966 declaration."

It is quite possible to do the same thing with language, always with the understanding that some outside factor may come along to knock the calculation into a cocked hat. One such factor in the development of the English language, for instance, was the Danish invasions of England before the Norman Conquest. As a result, today we say, "Take the knife and cut the steak" instead of "Nim the metter and sned the oxflesh," which would be the logical development of King Alfred's Anglo-Saxon without Scandinavian interference. Another factor was 1066 itself, by reason of which we say, "The army pays out large sums of money" instead of "The here tells out great tales of gild."

A projection of the English language into the future on the basis of present-day indications is something like the predictions of an IBM machine on election night when only the first two million votes are in. It can be fascinating, though many things may come along to upset our predictions. Nevertheless, despite the hazards, the questions can legitimately be asked: What can we prophesy at this moment about the English of one hundred years hence? How will our descendants of A.D. 2067 speak and write?

By looking at the changes that have taken place in the past, and at the way the language is changing now, I think we can make some reasonable predictions.

§   §   §

Let us first of all recall that language consists of sounds (or phonemes, sounds that are distinctively significant to the speakers); of grammatical forms (like *love, loves, loved,* or *see, sees, saw, seen,* or *child, children*); of word arrangements, like the characteristic "John kisses Mary," which indicates that John, coming before the verb, is the doer of the action, and Mary, coming after the verb, the recipient; and of individual words, laden with their distinctive meanings. Language change may and does occur in any of these four divisions: phonology, morphology, syntax, and vocabulary.

But the changes do not occur at the same rate or to the same extent in all four. In times of trouble and stress, when communities become isolated, or when an alien tongue comes in direct contact with the native language of an area, changes in sound and grammatical structure seem favored; when conditions are stable, sounds and grammar change moderately, but vocabulary grows quickly.

For this reason, the big sound-and-grammar changes in the English tongue took place primarily in the days of the Anglo-Saxons, the Danes, and the Normans, then again through the troublous times that preceded the stabilization of English society down to the reign of Queen Elizabeth I. There were numerous vocabulary changes in those days, too, but the most dramatic accretions in vocabulary have come since the dawn of the scientific era.

In the sounds of our language, the omens point to a process of stabilization and standardization, with local dialectal variants tending to be replaced by a uniform style of pronunciation. Indeed, it is likely that even the cleavage between British and American English will largely be effaced. There are many reasons for this. Huge centralized government units, easy communication between speakers of different areas, widespread trade and travel, and widespread education all favor unification and standardization. This was proved in the days of the Roman Empire, when a strong central government, good roads, unrestricted trade among the provinces, and a fairly good educational system (at least for that period) led to the use of a standardized Latin throughout the western part of the Empire, and a standardized Greek in the eastern regions. Today we have not only the American Union and the British Commonwealth, with their highly centralized features; we also have highways, railroads, swift ships, and jet planes, bringing the speakers of the various English-speaking areas into fast and easy contact with one another; we have public schooling for all social classes, with illiteracy practically eliminated; above all, we have the ubiquitous printing presses, radio, TV, and films, bringing a standard Queen's English and a standard general American to all readers, listeners, and viewers. The local dialects will probably never quite disappear; but they will be driven more and more underground. Only those mispronunciations that have spread throughout the country (*marjerine, heighth,* and *Febuary,* for instance; but not *boid, gyit, dem*) will come out on top. As for the cleavage between British and American English, the tendency has been toward reunification since World War I.

The pronunciation of the year 2067 will probably not differ too widely from the general American of our best radio and TV announcers today, blended with the Queen's English of the BBC. There will be an elimination of marked vulgarisms and localisms in pronunciation, which will be derided as old-fashioned (Cicero, writing in the first century B.C., used such expressions as *rustici dicebant,* "the rustics used to say" and *rustico sermone significabat,* "in rustic speech used to mean"; his use of the imperfect tense in this connection is a dead giveaway that these local forms of speech had gone out of fashion by his day).

In the matter of grammatical forms and arrangements,

our language today is far too standardized to permit of much change. It is possible that a few stray levelings may take place (*oxes, deers,* and *sheeps* for *oxen, deer,* and *sheep,* for instance; or *I heared him* for *I heard him;* or *I have drank* for *I have drunk*). But despite the widespread rantings of the apostles of usage (however that much-belabored word may be defined), it is not likely that substandard forms will make much headway. The primary reason for this is that such forms are usually in the nature of localisms. Such rank atrocities as "Them dogs are us'uns," "I seen the both'n of 'em," "I'll call you up without I can't," are too localized to survive the impact of schools and TV combined. The only grammatical changes that have a real chance of becoming part of the standard language are those of nationwide currency, such as "It's me," "Who did you see?", "between you and I," "these kind of books," "I seen him," "the data is," "he ain't been here." Judgment may be suspended for spelling-sound combinations like "I should of done it," and forms that lend themselves to jocular treatment, like "I should have stood in bed," "he hadn't ought to do it," or the satiric pseudo-commercial "We still brew good, like we used to could."

One historical factor that may blast our calculations to smithereens, however, is the possible development of a pidginized form of English for international use, and its reflected influence on the native speakers. If this happens, it is possible that we may get such analogical standardizations as *childs, mouses, gooses, foots* (so that all nouns may form their plurals the same way without exception), and *I did see, I did go* for *I saw, I went* (so that the basically simple English verb may be further simplified by having a universally regular past form).

§ § §

The really big changes will come in vocabulary: the proliferation of new words will make the English of 2067 a startlingly different language from that of today.

Here there are several factors at work. As man's activities

become increasingly complex and multiform, new words have to be coined, combined, borrowed, or otherwise created to take care of such activities. We have only to go over the list of vocabulary accretions since 1900 to realize what is in store for the language in the next hundred years. Think of *futurama, micromatic, motel, jitterbug, genocide, corny, snafu, gremlin, smog, zoot suit, mortician, marina, motorcade*—all words that would have stumped Dickens or Edgar Allan Poe. Add to these the specialized words of specialized fields (*megavolt* and *psychosomatic, positron* and *isotope, electronic* and *morphophonemic, kodak* and *latex, existentialism* and *zen, astronaut* and *cosmonaut, antibiotic* and *quasar, loran* and *feedback*). Consider also the words of older vintage now used in a variety of new acceptances (*atomic fission, featherbedding, integration, release, deceleration, satellite, twist, swing, liquidate, square, bromide*). Add to these our new word combinations where the meaning cannot be gathered from either of the component parts (*split level, fringe benefit, no-show, den mother, sit-in, baby-sitter, airlift, countdown, hard sell, point up, brainwashing, fallout, rock 'n' roll, loyalty oath, character assassination, namedropping, table hop, channel swimmer*). Continue with slang terms and coinages (*scram, jerk, boo-boo, schlemiel, footsie, beef up, goof, hood, stash, whiz, blurb, goop, boondoggle, globaloney, yakkety-yak, comeuppance, beatnik, palooka, schmo*). It is easy to see that the language of the future will be only partly comprehensible to the speaker of present-day English if things go on at this pace, even if the basic sounds, forms, sentence structures, and connecting words remain largely unchanged.

The future tongue would sound to present-day speakers somewhat like double-talk, or, better yet, those nonsense sentences that linguists often construct when they want to get away from meaning and concentrate on form—sentences in which the sounds, the grammatical forms, the word order, and the connecting words are all standard English, but in which the vocabulary is imaginary: something like "Foring mests larry no granning sunners in the rones." Or perhaps even more like authentic double-talk: "When the dummy was grogging with that jumbo rumpscuttle, they decided to run a rig with some gringo; but this old squawker blabbed to the Dogberry that the hot donna was a horse, and the stirk threw them out of the snuggery." Yet this weird vocabulary will of course be easily understood by speakers who have grown up with it.

§ § §

How many of our present, current, everyday words will be altogether obsolete or even archaic by 2067? A good many, no doubt. Look closely at the vocabulary of one hundred years ago and notice how many words were in current use then that we can still recognize, but would not think of using ourselves, words like *drawing-room* and *trencher, conscript* and *sparking light, eximious* and *mansuetude, scrimshaws* and *gardyloo, spinney* and *weald,* or, to go back a little farther, *vocular* and *viduous, gossipaceous* and *dandiacal.* If we care to go a few centuries further back, we can find *deruncinate* and *suppeditate, whirlicote* and *begeck, yuke* and *pringle, toom* and *mizzle, jarkmen* and *priggers, assation* and *clancular, dignotion* and *exolution.*

Since the language of radio and TV, in the English-speaking countries, is largely a matter of commercial promotion, a special word may be in order for the future ramifications of the Madison Avenue tongue.

In the field of sounds, the promotional language tends to avoid, save for occasional picturesque effect, localisms and special accents. This is perhaps one of the most powerful factors in the standardization we anticipate. Only occasionally do we get a deliberate distortion of pronunciation (*supphose*). In grammar and syntax, the language of promotion tends toward those vulgarisms that are nationwide ("Us Tareyton smokers would rather fight than switch" is a good example), but not toward local or extreme forms.

In the advertising vocabulary, two contradictory trends

have been noted. One is the tendency to stress the short, pithy, monosyllabic elements of vocabulary at the expense of longer, more "educated" words (*Fab, Tide, Joy*). But side by side with this, we have droves of commercialized scientific and pseudoscientific words designed to dazzle the prospective buyer (*hydromatic* and *foot-o-matic, irradiated, duridium, dura-drive, vibra-free, Toronado*).

In the field of grammar, perhaps the most objectionable tendency of the advertising language is that of conferring upon nouns a phony functional change whereby they are compared as though they were adjectives (to exaggerate somewhat: "Yummies are yummier, crummies are crummier, tummies are tummier, because coffee is coffier, or coffeyer, or even coffee-er"). This, coupled with the tiresome repetition of the name of the sponsor or the product, and the concomitant elimination of "it" and "they" from the language, may yet turn out to be Madison Avenue's biggest contribution to the language of the twenty-first century.

§   §   §

But all in all, despite the multiplying of human activity, the advances of science and of its nomenclature, and the ravages of commercialism, it seems to me that we are not justified in expecting too radical a change in the language, particularly in its sound-and-grammar structure, in the course of the next hundred years, provided present trends continue. This picture may be drastically changed by the unexpected or the unforeseeable, however. A historical upset, a political upheaval, a military disaster may place the English language in swift motion once more, so that a century or two could bring on the same differences that appear between the Anglo-Saxon of Aelfric and the Middle English of Chaucer.

CHAPTER TWENTY-FIVE

A B C D E F G H I J K L M N O P Q R S T U V W X Y Z

2075: A Flight of the Imagination

Even before he opened his eyes, George Forsyth began remembering. It was as though it had all happened yesterday, but he knew it was much, much farther back than yesterday. He, like the other nine volunteers of the Rockford Foundation, had climbed into his hibernation casket, lain down, closed his eyes to the lulling sound of the soft music. Then he had drifted off into nothingness. A pleasant nothingness, studded with dreams of which he could remember no part. Now he heard the same soft strains to which he had gone to sleep. But there was more; voices talking in subdued tones. The inflection sounded a little British to his ears. There were words he couldn't hear, others he couldn't understand, but for this he was prepared.

He finally opened his eyes, as the talking ceased. The room was different from the one in which he had gone to sleep. It was circular, with a rounded ceiling. The light was subdued, but he could not see its source. If there were doors and windows, they were concealed.

The man who stood over him was rather young, with blue eyes, a ruddy complexion, brown hair, and a wisp of a mustache. He wore a white tunic, with sleeves cut off at the elbow and an open neck. He was smiling pleasantly.

"Welcome to the twenty-first century, Mr. Forsyth!" he

said cheerfully, in his clipped British accent. "So nice to see that you have come down to us safe and sound!"

"You know all about it?" asked George, a little breathlessly.

"Yes, of course! Quite an idea, and we're carrying it on. We put ten men into hibernation last month. Your own companions are going to sleep on for quite a while, as you know. I'm afraid you won't manage to speak to any of them. But with you back in the land of the living, we're getting off to a grand start. Why don't you rest a little longer before you get up?"

George was in no hurry to leave his comfortable casket. After one hundred years, what were a few minutes more or less? Besides, he wanted to think and get his bearings.

"This is the year 2075?" he asked.

"Right! We got you out right on the dot. May 20th, in your reckoning. The calendar has been reformed a bit, but you needn't worry about that now. The others go on every hundred years. Your last companion will come back to life in 2975. Grand idea of your Rockford people, to give each subsequent century a firsthand glimpse into yours by supplying a living informant. Best possible historical source. Our scientists and scholars are all waiting to interrogate you, but that will come later. First we have to get you adjusted to your new surroundings."

George sighed. "Have things changed—much?" he asked.

"Mostly for the better. At least we like to think so. But you will see for yourself. I have been delegated to initiate you. I am 236–01–964."

He held out his hand, and George took it. There seemed to be no trace of muscular atrophy. "But what is your name?" he asked.

"Well, this is your first shock. We abandoned names back in 2005, and gave everybody a single number instead. That takes care of everything—vital statistics, identification, Social Security, bank accounts, credit cards, even family relations.

Most convenient, you know. I've often wondered how you people managed to keep track of all the names and numbers you had."

George was making mental notes. His primary interest came to the fore. "How about the language?" he asked. "You seem to talk the way I do, but you were speaking to someone before I opened my eyes, and some of the words sounded strange."

"Oh, that has changed, to be sure. But of course they picked a specialist in twentieth-century English to take care of you. Whenever I use an unfamiliar word, don't hesitate to stop me and ask. You have to be brought up to date, you know."

"Are you British?" asked George.

The man laughed. "Goodness, no! I was born and raised here in New York. The two languages got closer and closer, and finally they merged, just as the nations did. I sound a bit British to you, but if you were a twentieth-century Englishman, I'd sound like an American."

George lay and pondered. "May I get up now?" he inquired.

"You certainly may. I'm anxious to start you on your rounds. We won't try to take in too much at first. I'll just take you home for dinner and put you to bed. Tomorrow we'll really start indoctrinating you and pumping you for information. You'll have a pleasant life in our world, I think."

George climbed slowly out of his casket. But there was no need for caution. His muscles were perfectly pliant and responsive, his senses keen, his mind clear as a bell.

"Here, get out of that sheet and put on these clothes," said 236–01–964. He held out a costume quite similar to his own. White, half-sleeved, open-necked tunic that came halfway down to the knees, loose-fitting white pants with elastic belt, white shoes made of some soft, comfortable material with zipper fasteners. "Is this all we wear?" George asked, a little suspiciously.

"We don't need anything else. We have weather control now. The temperature, inside and out, is always an even seventy degrees, on your old Fahrenheit scale. Rain only when we want it, and always late at night. By the way, you can shorten my number to the last three figures. Call me 964. That's about the same as using a person's first name back in your century."

964 had taken George by the hand. Now he was leading him toward one point of the circular room. "Before we leave the building," he said, "I'd like to take you over to the viewing room and show you three very short films. We prepared them especially for you, as a sort of cultural and linguistic introduction, before your real training starts. They'll give you some idea of what you are going to be up against in the matter of language and customs. Also, you'll see some scenes that will interest you. It will only take ten minutes. I'll explain each film after you've seen it."

They seemed to be walking straight into a blank wall, but when they were a yard away the wall suddenly parted. An empty corridor lay beyond. "Don't look so surprised!" 964 laughed. "After all, you had electric-eye doors even back in 1975! We've just made them a little less conspicuous and a little more convenient."

The corridor was long, well lighted with the same soft, subdued, invisible light that had illuminated the room where George had awakened from his long slumber. There were seemingly no doors, but at one point 964 faced right and took two steps toward the wall. Again it parted. They found themselves in another room, larger than the first, fitted with what seemed to be form-contour chairs spaced at intervals. George was motioned into one of these. 964 reclined in another, then held up his hand. The light grew dim, and a screen suddenly appeared at the far end of the room.

"The first thing you're going to see," said 964, "is a brief political announcement. Yes, we still have politics. I don't think we've made too much improvement in that field since your time. But see for yourself."

The screen suddenly lit up, though no camera or operator was visible. It showed a scene that reminded George of a baseball stadium. People in large numbers sat, tier upon tier, their attention fixed upon a figure standing on a raised platform in the center of the stadium, surrounded by batteries of microphones. Both speaker and audience were clad in the white half-sleeved tunics that were evidently standard in this century. The women, George noted with curiosity, were attired exactly like the men, but wore their hair long, in neat knots on top of their heads. All looked reasonably healthy and happy, but their behavior was noticeably more subdued than that of the old crowds at political gatherings. The man on the podium was speaking, and all were listening intently. His voice at first came in a jumble of sound to George's ears, then suddenly grew loud and clear.

"248–20–766 is a sophocrat who thinks there ought to be heavy free rolls in every city lane," the speaker was saying. "What happens to your mercs if he's lec? Opt for 711–21–304! A real prac, a real ec, and a real uni! He's the unicrat this town needs!"

The voice faded away, the screen disappeared, and the soft light was again diffused through the room.

"Now," said 964 with a smile, "let's analyze what you heard. You already know that we all go by number, not by name. 'Heavy,' which was an adjective in your day, got to be used with the meaning of 'much,' 'many,' 'lots of.' 'Rolls' are the endless moving platforms with seats we have on some of our main streets for local, short-distance traffic. They were fashioned after your escalators, and supply cheap rapid transit. They are graded in four speeds, and you move yourself from one speed-track to another according to your hurry and the distance you have to go. But you buy a token to get on. 248–20–766 is what you might have called an advanced liberal. We call them sophocrats. He is running for the post of unicrat, which more or less coincides with your mayor.

He pledges that if he is elected (notice that we have cut that down to 'lec') he will install free rolls not only in the main streets, but even in the cross streets, or lanes. That will obviously take lots of 'mercs,' which is our currency ('mercury' is the full name for the unit that represents a blend of the dollar and the pound). The speaker was urging the 'opters,' or voters, to opt for 711–21–304, who has conservative tendencies. He is, as you heard, a 'prac' (practical man), an 'ec' (economics expert), and a real 'uni' (that's our general term for leader); 'unident' is the President, 'unicrat' the local mayor; the separate states, with their governors, passed out of existence just about half a century ago. Any questions?"

George had been taking mental notes. He shook his head. "No, I think I can remember all of it. It would help if I could write it down."

"You won't need any written notes," said his mentor. "It's all inscribed in this little microvox, which is yours. Just press the button, and you can listen to the three recordings as long and as often as you like."

He handed George a tiny object that resembled a box of headache pills. "Just keep it in your pocket, and use it whenever you like."

"But don't you write any more?" asked George.

"Oh, yes, but only when it's necessary, which isn't very often. Later I'll give you a textbook to go with your microvoxes. By the way, you'll find that the spelling has changed. But your record says you were a language specialist, and our present writing is based on your International Phonetic Alphabet. You'll have no trouble with it. Shall we take the second film?"

The light grew dim again, the screen reappeared. This time George saw two men seated in what looked like the cockpit of an airplane or helicopter. The vehicle was in rapid motion, flying rather low over cornfields and clumps of trees. The two men wore helmets, but were otherwise attired in the universal white tunic and pants. They were talking excitedly to each other. Their voices grew suddenly clear.

"Hit that upping lever, 245! We can't use our megabane than on those beats! If we do we'll thane all the fliers!"

"Who are you telling? I'm the astrogator here!"

"Sure you are! But what do you know about zoobio?"

The voices faded out, as did the image.

"Those," said 964, "are two air-rangers in a scooter-plane. They belong to the Bureau of Fields, Farms, and Waterways, and they were sent out to exterminate insect pests. 'Beats' is short for beatles, which got to be the general name for all insects after some popular singers adopted it back in your time. The air-rangers use a spray-gun which has a long Greek name, 'thanatodoser,' or 'death-giver'; but it's usually abbreviated to 'than,' with unvoiced *th;* we've even formed a verb on its stem, 'to thane,' which means to kill off. 'Megabane' is a hybrid insecticide; 'big' in Greek, 'destruction' in Anglo-Saxon. "Fliers" is our word for "birds," which gradually acquired an obscene meaning and was dropped from polite circulation. Try to remember not to use it, at least in mixed company."

"Yes," mused George, "I remember the transformation was starting in my day, and it was already in full swing in some other languages, like Italian. I can figure out "zoobio" as animal biology, and "astrogator" is probably a pilot."

964 nodded. "Yes, at first we used it only for spacemen to other planets; then it got to be jokingly used for any kind of pilot, even on a scooter-plane. The term is reported to have first been coined back around 1950 by a science-fiction writer, Hugo Gernsback. Did you ever hear of him, or come across the word?"

George shook his head. "No, I'm afraid not. What's an 'upping lever'?"

"Our scooter-planes are equipped with upping and downing levers if you want to go up or down vertically. Not too different from the old helicopters. But they can also fly horizontally at five hundred miles an hour. Our big transocean planes can hit speeds of three thousand miles an hour. Less than two hours to Moscow, if you could only land there."

"You mean we're still having trouble with the Soviets?"

"Not real trouble. Just a little cold war once in a while. But we can't stray off on international politics. I'll fill you in on that later. Ready for the last film? This is going to be real good. That's why I saved it for the last. You're going to get some authentic twenty-first-century slang."

The screen glowed again. This time the scene seemed to be a room in a private home: the usual circular arrangement, with arched ceiling, and no visible doors or windows. But there were several comfortable-looking low-contour chairs and sofas, a number of strange-looking cabinets, and something resembling carpeting on the floor. A young girl (she must be a teen-ager, George thought) was lying on her stomach on one of the sofas, reading a picture magazine in brilliant colors. She was rather attractive, despite the fact that she wore the customary tunic and had her hair in a tuft on top of her head. Suddenly she got up, walked to one of the cabinets, and pressed a button. The cabinet's doors slid open, revealing a television screen. The girl fumbled with a knob at the side of the cabinet. On the screen a boy's face appeared, blond, not bad-looking, and quite young.

"Hello, 345–8!" cooed the girl. "Yes, 8, 8!" The boy said something, but George could not catch it. "I wanted to tell you," the girl went on somewhat breathlessly, "last night I saw our friend 653 . . . What's that? . . . No, Moose, not 745–88–653! 907–34–653! . . . Sure you know her. She was telling me that you and 988–76–583 are going twin, and that you're planning to get yoked. I told her she was beany. It's you and me! . . . Shhh . . . I got to cut. I hear he-senior coming in! Heavy osc! See you tonight at the disc! Jalapoom-wah!"

The image on the cabinet screen faded out, but not soon enough. George's own screen caught a silent door opening and a man striding in—none other than his own mentor,

964. He looked sternly at the girl and wagged an accusing finger. She blushed and hung her head. Then 964 spoke:

"Come on, 211! Halt that kassick frimping, and deviz that twist you met in your ungregged brain-fac!"

The image on the screen broke into a grin as the screen faded out and the light came on. George looked at his companion and saw that he was shaking with silent merriment.

"How's that for a family scene? 211 is my own daughter, and I thought I'd get her to put on an act with me for your benefit. Not that the situation isn't real; it's real enough! She's sixteen, and she attends what the younger generation call a 'brain-fac' or 'brain-factory'; in other words, a high school. Some brain-facs are sexgregated, other are what you people called co-ed; we call them 'ungregged,' short for 'unsexgregated.' There she met this twist; you might have used 'jerk' in your day. I was telling her to deviz (or devisualize) him. That's a word with *double entente:* it means to turn off the image on your televisionphone, but also to put somebody out of your thoughts."

"I can figure 'halt' for 'stop,' " said George, "but what did you mean by 'kassick frimping'?"

" 'Kassick' is an abbreviated form of 'jackassical.' It's a nice, useful word. I don't think you had it. 'To frimp' is a blend of 'frown' and 'simper.' Did you notice the extra number 8 she used when she called him up? That's our equivalent of your affectionate diminutive, a figure of endearment, like 'darling' or 'honey.' 'Moose' is another pet word girls use for boys. Of course you got 'going twin' and 'getting yoked.' You used to 'go steady' and 'get spliced,' or 'hitched.' But 'to get married' is still used in adult circles. You also got 'beany' for 'crazy.' 'Senior' is what they call the parent nowadays. 'Heavy osc' means "lots of kisses' (osculation, you know), and 'disc' is short for 'discothèque.' Yes, we still have them. We'll get 211 to take us to one, so you can admire our popular music and dancing."

"What was that last word she used when she devized him?" asked George.

"Jalapoomwah? Just teen-age talk for 'bye-bye,' 'see you later.' But it changes every year or so. Well, that about ends your indoctrination for the day. How about going home, meeting 211 and her she-senior, and having some dinner? We can ride the rolls. It isn't far from here."

They rose from their viewing seats and walked toward the wall. "By the way," said 964, taking George's arm familiarly as the invisible door opened before them, "don't be too surprised to see so many scooter-planes flying low over the streets and rolls. They're perfectly safe. They are all atomic-powered, and equipped with radar that prevents them from colliding. Oh, another thing! Most of us still eat, but just for pleasure. Our nourishment comes in a single capsule that we take every morning when we wake up. But the M.D.'s thought our digestive tracts would deteriorate too rapidly if we stopped using them all at once, and give rise to other disturbances, so they advised us to keep on eating—those of us that could afford it, at any rate. But don't be surprised if 211 just sits and watches us. She worries about her figure."

They had been walking down the silent, empty corridor. Now 964 turned right. A door slid open. From outside came the hum of many voices and many motors.

Arm in arm with his mentor, George Forsyth stepped out into the strange new world of 2075.

A NOTE ABOUT THE AUTHOR

Mario Pei was born in Rome, Italy, in 1901. He came to the United States in 1908 and was educated in New York schools: St. Francis Xavier High School, City College (where he was elected to Phi Beta Kappa), and Columbia University, where he received his Ph.D. in 1932. At the age of seventeen he began his teaching career as a grade teacher in the St. Francis Xavier Grammar School. He was instructor in Romance languages at City College from 1923 to 1937. At Columbia University he has been assistant professor of Romance languages, 1937–47; associate professor, 1947–52; and since 1952, professor of Romance philology. Professor Pei is recognized as one of the foremost authorities on language today. He has written extensively for professional journals and general magazines and has lectured widely. During World War II he created a thirty-seven-language course in War Linguistics at Columbia University and collaborated with OSS and OWI in the preparation of linguistic projects connected with the war effort. More recently, he was linguistic consultant at the U. S. Army Language School in Monterey, California, and NATO exchange lecturer at the University of Lisbon, Portugal. He is the author of many widely read books, including *Invitation to Linguistics, How to Learn Languages and What Languages to Learn, The Story of Language* (a Book-of-the-Month Club selection), and *The Story of English.*

A NOTE ON THE TYPE

The text of this book has been set in a type face called "Basker-ville." The face is a facsimile reproduction of type cast from molds made for JOHN BASKERVILLE (1706–1775) from his designs. The punches for the revived Linotype Baskerville were cut under the supervision of the English printer George W. Jones.

John Baskerville's original face was one of the forerunners of the type style known as "modern face" to printers: a "modern" of the period A.D. 1800.

The book was composed, printed, and bound by The Book Press Incorporated, Brattleboro, Vermont. Typography and binding designs by Kenneth Miyamoto.